A CURIOUS
HISTORY OF CATS

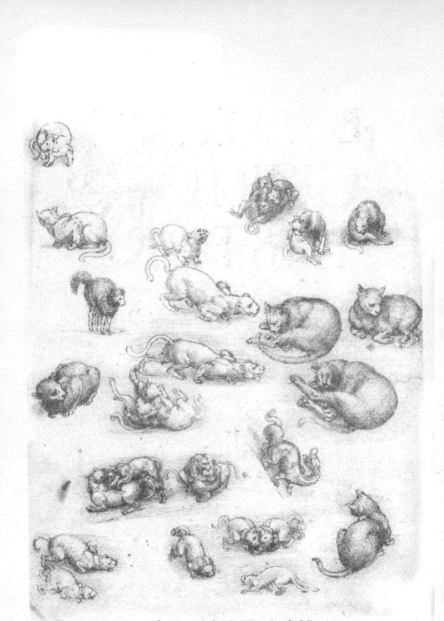

Twenty-seven Cats and a Dragon, by Leonardo da Vinci
(1507–1508)

A
CURIOUS
HISTORY
OF CATS

Madeline Swan

In loving memory of Jasper,
who watched over me
like a wise, whiskery old sage
as I wrote this book.

First published in the United Kingdom in 2007 by Little Books Ltd.
This edition published in 2015 by Max Press.

10 9 8 7 6 5 4 3 2 1

Text copyright © 2015 by Madeline Swan
Design and layout copyright © 2015 by Little Books Ltd
Jacket Ilustrations © James Nunn

A CIP catalogue record for this book is available from the British Library.

ISBN: 978 1 906251 73 4

The author and publisher will be grateful for any information that will assist
them in keeping future editions up-to-date. Although all reasonable care has been
taken in the preparation of this book, neither the publisher, editors nor the author
can accept any liability for any consequences arising from the use thereof, or the
information contained therein.

Printed and bound by CPI Group (UK) Ltd

CONTENTS

Introduction 9

1 Cats of Ancient History, Myth & Religion 17

2 Cats as Deity in Ancient Egypt,
Greece & Rome 33

3 Medieval Cats of Lore & Legend 57

4 Devillish Cats & Centuries of Persecution 83

5 Tudor, Shakespearean & Stuart Cats
of Mixed Fortune 103

6 Georgian Literary Cats of
Elegance & Devotion 133

7 Some Literary & Artistic Cats
of the Romantic Age 151

8 Victorian Cats & Owners of Distinction 179

9 Working Cats, Cats of Luxury
& Decadence in Modern Times 211

Great Cat Lovers & Haters 247

Select Bibliography 252

Acknowledgments

The author and publishers wish to thank the following individuals, museums and libraries for their kind permission to reproduce their material. Every effort has been taken to trace copyright owners. However, if any have been overlooked we send our apologies and will, if informed, rectify all future reprints and editions. Unless otherwise stated, all black and white line drawings have been taken from the original publications, as listed in the Bibliography on pages 252 and 253.

p. 41, *The Gods and their Creators*, by Edwin Long, The Art Archive;
ps 44 and 45 Wild cats from *The Year of the Tiger*, 1569, The British Library;
p. 48 *Ipuy and his Wife*, restored by N. de G. Davies, 1920, The Metropolitan Museum of Art;
p. 71, *Adoration of the Angels and the Three Magi*, by Benozzo de Lesse, The Art Archive;
p. 73, *Aristotelis Naturalis*, The British Library;
p. 75 drawing of a cat by Michaelangelo, Dover Publications; drawing by Leonardo da Vinci from a selection held by HM the Queen at Windsor;
p. 81, *Whittington and his Cat*, The British Library;
p. 84, domestic cat taken from the *Natural History of Four Footed Beasts* by Edward Topsell;
p. 89 detail from *Joseph in Prison* by the Master of the Story of Joseph, Harris Brisbane Dick Fund, The Metropolitan Museum of Art;
p. 92, *The Love Potion*, by Evelyn de Morgan, The De Morgan Centre, London/www.bridgeman.co.uk;
p. 110, wooden panel by Hans Süss von Kulmbach, J. Pierpont Morgan;
p. 115, Cardinal Richelieu and his cats, *Les Animaux Historiques*, 21436, The British Library;
p. 127, *Girl with a Kitten*, Jean-Baptiste Perronneau, The Art Archive;
p. 128, *Kitten*, by George Stubbs, The British Library;
p. 141, *Cat with Butterfly*, 186331, Or.14391, The British Library;

p. 146, *The Cat of Kazan*, The Art Archive;
p. 165 *Sleeping Cat*, private collection;
p. 166, *Musk-rat Raja*, 001434, Add. or 3351, The British Library;
p. 171, *Winter Quarters*, by Paton and Allais, The Art Archive;
p.s 174 and 175, *White Cats Watching Goldfish*, by Arthur Heyer, Stern Art Dealers, London, UK; www. bridgeman.co.uk;
p. 178, *At Home: A Portrait*, by Walter Crane, Leeds Museums and Galleries (City Art Gallery) UK/www.bridgeman.co.uk;
p. 191, *Kitten and Ball of Wool*, by Murato Kokuda, The Art Archive;
p. 194, *Kitten*, by Charles van den Eyken, private collection;
p. 209, *Tinkie*, by Derold Page, Derold Page/www.bridgeman.co.uk;
p. 210, *Cat with Butterfly*, by Lyn Hemmant, Lyn Hemmant/The Art Archive;
p. 213, *Cat in the Window of a Cottage*, by Ralph Hedley, private collection;
ps 217 and 223, *Lait pur de la Vingeanne Sterilise* and *Tournée du Chat Noir*, by Théophile Steinlen, copyright Dover Publications;
p. 227, *Cat*, by Tsugouharu Leonard Foujita, private collection, www.bridgeman.co.uk and DACS;
p. 245, Persian cat, by Harrison Weir, and p. 246, postcard by Louis Wain both courtesy of Celia Haddon

'Like those great sphinxes lounging through
eternity in noble attitudes upon the desert
sand, they gaze in curiosity at nothing,
calm and wise.'

Charles Baudelaire (1821-1867)
Les Chats, Spleen et Idéal,
Les Fleurs du Mal, 1857

INTRODUCTION

Once upon a time there was a small dull-coated tabby cat that lived in the wild away from mankind. She lived with her kittens and spent time with a series of small tom cats that passed by when she was on season and sometimes stayed a little while. A carnivore, she caught mice, lizards and even insects.

Several thousand years later there was a curious change. Her offspring were being housed, fed and entertained by humans. They no longer hunted for their food. Instead they ate lavish meals out of tins or packets. It was the humans who went out to hunt for them by shopping in supermarkets and bringing home food.

Instead of dens in hollow trees or rocks or banks, the cats sprawled on humans' soft beds or napped in specially designed furry cat beds. In winter the humans heated the whole house for them and in summer put on the air conditioning so they would not get too hot. The cats came in all sorts of colours – black, white, ginger, tortoiseshell and many others.

There was no more caterwauling and sex under the stars with passing stray toms. These descendants, mainly neutered and spayed, no longer had kittens, or, if they did, they were the result of careful liaisons, nuptials arranged by anxious human carers after consulting pedigrees.

How did this happen? This light-hearted narrative gives some of the highlights of feline history – the curious ups and downs of cats through the ages. It tells the tale of individual mousers who made it into the human record – in literature, in history and even very occasionally in warfare (human, of course!).

When dogs entered man's society they hung around groups of humans, eating their rubbish. But soon they began to earn their living by obeying orders, helping humans hunt, and guarding their homes. As well as being man's best friend, they became his obedient helper.

Cats, however, did nothing of the kind. They kept their independence. They may have moved in to man's society to eat the rats and mice among the rubbish and, when man began to practise agriculture, they helped protect the grain stores against mice by hunting and eating them, but they never took orders as dogs did. You could say they exploited human society, rather than being exploited like so many other domestic animals.

Of course, some cats took up a kind of semi-official employment in agriculture, brewing, the Civil Service and the Post Office. This book tells the tale of several working cats. Yet most of them were just pets and at the beginning of this century most humans in Europe and the USA no longer insisted on their cats earning their living by catching mice.

Modern cats are not like modern dogs, they do not do obedience or teamwork. There are so far no sniffer cats, no police cats, no hearing or guide cats, and few, if any, guard cats. Attempts to train them in this way have proved futile.

In the world of the cat, the cat's duty is to take graciously from the human and the human's duty is to give conscientiously to the cat. Perhaps the most glorious moment in cat history was their time in ancient Egypt. From a wild desert animal they became gods, objects of veneration and worship.

From this high point, their delicate relationship with mankind went downhill. They held their place in human society as pest control operatives but refused to jeopardise their integrity by taking orders. In the hierarchical society of the Middle Ages, then later in the turbulent seventeenth century, this cost them dear. They became objects of suspicion to some people.

Human society persecuted witches and with them their cats by burning, skinning alive, and drowning the creatures. It was during the nineteenth century that the unjust lowly status of cats began to reverse. Queen Victoria, herself, intervened to make sure that the RSPCA logo of the time included a cat, not just a dog. Cats, as well as dogs, began to feature in children's books as objects of love. My favourite is the verse that goes:

> 'D is for Dog, Faithful and True,
> I hope he gets married to Pussy, don't you?'

Cat shows, in which cats were divided into different races, came into being at Crystal Palace in July 16 1871. The artist Harrison Weir felt that only by creating pedigree cats could their status be enhanced so that they gained an equality with dogs. He divided them by colour – tabbies, tortoiseshells, for example – by fur length and by ancestry – Russian, Siamese, Manx and so forth.

While this may, as it did for dogs, raise the status of cats, it was to have severe consequences for cat welfare a century or so later. The restricted gene pool of pedigree matings, added to the unwise decisions of some judges, has led to mis-shapen bodies and some very unpleasant hereditary diseases. The result is that the inbred pedigree cat is sometimes physically and emotionally worse off than the stray in the streets.

The other great step forward in cat history was the invention of spaying female cats. Tom cats had always been neutered just as farm animals were, but females had had to go through the business of perpetual kitten bearing, producing as many as 200 in a lifetime. These unwanted kittens were usually drowned and it was the mark of a kind owner in Victorian times to let their female cat rear just one of the litter.

Mrs Nearea de Clifford, one of the early members of the charity, Cats Protection, recalled her vet tentatively suggesting the operation in 1946. Soon the charity adopted and promoted the idea. Birth control for cats had finally arrived and was a huge breakthrough in cat welfare.

Yet there are still welfare implications for the pampered pet of this century. Indoor cats, deprived of the opportunity for natural behaviour like hunting, may suffer from boredom and obesity. If their human owners are out all day, these cats are at risk of becoming prisoners in solitary confinement. In the USA cats have their claws removed by veterinary operations, saving the furniture at the cost of their chance to climb and claw as nature intended them to do.

Finally, even the world of cat rescuers, who do so much good work, can be perverted into mere animal collection. Compulsive rescuers may become collectors. They take in too many cats and may not have the funds to keep them properly. Unvaccinated cats lead to a household of diseased animals. Moreover, since cats are not pack animals, some live in conditions of great stress and unhappiness from overcrowding.

So we must not be self-satisfied about how we keep our cats. The history of the cat shows us that some of the so-called improvements in animal welfare may have their unintended consequences. Human beings have an infinite capacity to persuade themselves that what is convenient or pleasurable for them, is also good for their cats. Often they are wrong.

For cats remain cats and prefer to lead a feline, not a human life. Indoor pedigree cats, deprived of the sight of a mouse, will quickly adapt to hunting if somebody is kind enough to let them out into a wider world. Happy cats, given a cat flap, come and go as they choose. They have an independent life of their own condescending only to share part of it with their self-styled owners.

All in all, cats are great survivors – as their curious history shows. They have adapted well to the twenty-first century. They keep their independence and, if they don't like what is happening at home, will leave to find a better owner. They make their preferences clear, as the pet food manufacturers know. While they cannot go out and shop for their own food, they are capable of training their humans to select the right brand.

Cats have never forgotten those years in ancient Egypt. If you look into the unblinking eyes of your cat, you will see its ancestral memories of being worshipped by humans. Most cats are friendly and loving, but there is in the friendship just a flicker of condescension. They have no doubt that humans are the inferior species and, looking round at the world we have made, perhaps they are right.

Detail from: *The Village of Eight Bridges at Okazaki*, by Utagawa
Kunisada (1786-1865).

Chapter I

CATS OF ANCIENT HISTORY, MYTH & RELIGION

The ancestors of the household cat that has an honoured place today beside many sitting room fires are descended from a beast that roamed the world more than fifty million years ago. The beast, known as the 'miacis' was the forebear not only of cats, but of bears, weasels and cat's traditional enemy, the dog. The first true cats, more like lynxes than today's moggies, Persians or Siamese, have been around for over ten million years. Modern cats similar to the domestic ones that are family pets, stalk the streets or hunt a farmer's rats, are descended from wild cats about four thousand years ago.

Once the cat became domesticated in Egypt it spread to other lands comparatively rapidly. It was soon a common sight in Greece, Rome and the adjoining Mediterranean lands. From these countries seafarers carried cats along trade routes throughout the world. In time they became established in every country and continent other than in Antarctica.

Although cats were valued because they had a role protecting crops and houses from rodents, they were also prized both for their beauty and as companions in the house. There is some debate about the time at which cats became domesticated in each country and this must remain a subject for discussion as there is very little evidence from archaeological remains.

Wild cats from Egypt spread into India where they also later became domesticated. Some scholars believe that they reached India from Egypt via the Middle East, but most subscribe to the theory that ancient Phoenician traders were responsible for carrying them to the Far East. Phoenician traders also later took the Manx cat to Britain and the ordinary domestic cat to the ports on the Cornish, Devon and Western coasts.

The spread of the cat beyond Europe, Asia and Africa to America and Australasia was much later. Some cats, enlisted for their mouse-catching prowess aboard ship, slipped ashore in the Americas. Others were brought, as late as the eighteenth century, by the European settlers both as pets and to control the local vermin population. It was the Spanish colonists who took their cats to South America and the French and

British who introduced them to North America. A hundred and fifty years later the ships of the first fleet were instrumental in introducing the cats they were carrying to Australia.

No sooner had the cat established itself away from the Middle East, it became part of the folklore and legend of its new territories. In Assam the village elders still tell of the time when a cat lived with his brother, the tiger. Legend has it that the tiger became sick, began to shiver and realised that he needed a fire to keep warm and that only man knew how to build a fire. To help his brother, the cat approached a house in order to seek help, but there was no one at home. Instead, there was some fish and rice on the floor. The cat could not resist. After eating the fish he went to take a nap by the fire and only on waking remembered his purpose, whereupon he took a burning stick in his mouth and returned to his friend. As the tiger grew stronger, the cat revealed that he had discovered a new way of life and was going to live in the house of man where he could be sure of food and warmth. So, legend has it, the cat became domesticated.

In China, cats have always been revered as a symbol of good fortune. There are portraits still in existence of noble Chinese families living more than a thousand years ago, from the Sung Dynasty (960-1279), in which cats have been included with their masters and mistresses.

At about the same time Emperor Ichijo of Japan (986-1011), still only thirteen years old, reared a litter of kittens at the Imperial Palace in Tokyo. The kittens were fed only the best food (including rice) and even given clothes to wear and a wet nurse named Uma No Myobu, to look after them. A local dog dared to chase one of the Emperor's adored cats. The Emperor was enraged. The dog was banished and its owner jailed. The Emperor continued to import expensive house-trained cats from China. These became the favourites of the Japanese ruling class, and were treated initially as treasured possessions, especially prized as they had been presented by the Emperor. The more Emperor Ichijo came to know his cats, the more he loved them.

Cats soon worked their way into ancient Japanese folklore where their role was a rather menacing one. The tale is still told of a demon cat, the Vampire Cat of Nabeshima. It is said that this cat killed a beautiful maiden by biting her neck. Assuming her identity in human form, the cat then fell prey on her lover, sucking his blood and causing him to weaken. In the end the prince's friend and companion came to his aid, and the beast was hunted and destroyed. An alternative legend of the Vampire Cat later arose in Spain in the form of a large black cat named 'El Broosha'. El Broosha was believed to appear in the dead of night and to suck the blood from sleeping babies in their cots.

Whatever the true origin of the Siamese, it is certain that for many hundreds of years the sacred role of the animal has been central to the religious life of the Siam people. It is therefore not surprising that the Siamese has always been regarded as a cat of high social breeding, confined to the Royal Palace in Siam and many noble homes belonging to the Siamese aristocracy as well as in the holy temples of the region. The *Thong Daeng* or 'Copper', an ancient Siamese domestic cat appearing in the manuscripts known as *The Cat Book Poems* is thought to be the ancestor of the Burmese cat.

There exists a number of theories regarding the origins of the Siamese cat, although there is no hard evidence. Some scholars say that ancient Egyptian traders carried their cats to the Orient, where they gradually developed into the Siamese breed. Others say that the Siamese is descended from an Oriental wild cat species. Another story has it that as recently as the twentieth century a rare and treasured white cat of great beauty was presented to the King of Siam as a special gift and from this animal the Siamese breed developed through inter-breeding with darker temple cats. Another holds that several hundred years ago there was a natural mutation in the cats of Siam, resulting in the dark-pointed markings on its fur.

According to ancient Islamic tradition the Prophet Muhammad was a great lover of cats. It is said that he would preach to his companions with a cat in his arms. Another example of the Prophet's admiration for the cat is the nickname that he chose for 'Abd ar-Rahman ad-Dawsi, one of his favourite companions. 'Abd ar-Rahman was greatly revered as one of those men who collected the sayings of the Prophet Muhammad, who respected his ability and was also impressed on one occasion when he saw 'Abd ar-Rahman being especially kindly towards a kitten. From then on the Prophet named him 'Abu Hurayrah', which means 'Father of the Kitten'.

On another occasion the Prophet was resting and a cat came and sat down beside him and went to sleep on his cloak. In time the Prophet needed to move and rather than wake the cat, cut away that part of his garment on which the cat continued to sleep. When the Prophet returned home at the end of the day the great warmth of the welcome he received from the cat so delighted him that he decreed that from then onwards cats should be specially treated. It is said that the cat awoke and bowed his head in gratitude, upon which the Prophet stroked him three times, allowing him a permanent place in paradise.

Another tradition reports that Muhammad was once saved by a cat from a deadly snake that had crept into his sleeve. The cat asked the snake to show its head, and when it appeared, carried it away. From that time onwards, cats have been treated with kindness and love in Islamic culture.

Long before Muhammad's death in the seventh century AD cats had already become treasured animals in the lands of Arabia. Although there are many theories existing as to the origin of the Persian cat, some scholars have argued that longhaired cats did indeed originate from the territory of central Asia now known as Iran.

One legend has it that as long ago as 525BC the Persians, led by King Cambyses, were involved in a ferocious battle for Pelesium in Egypt. It seemed certain that the Egyptians would beat off the Persians and win the day. The Persian leaders decided that the tide could only be turned if they could think up a ruse to match that of the wooden horse of Troy. The

Persians were aware that the Egyptians considered cats sacred and would do nothing to harm them, so they scoured the countryside for cats, any cats that they could find. Every Persian soldier was issued with a cat and on the day of the battle, when the soldiers charged the Egyptian force, a cat was in the arms of each of the advancing Persians. Not one Egyptian solder dared to take any action that could risk the life of a divine creature and the Persians won the day.

The same legend is sometimes recounted rather differently. It is said that the Persian soldiers gathered together not only cats, but dogs and any other animals that had a place in the religious rites of Egypt, and they were driven ahead of the Persian army.

There are many theories and scant evidence for the origin of the longhair, or Persian cat we know in modern times. Hermann Dembreck speaks of one possible theory, based on the time following the Persian conquest at Pelesium. Dembreck writes that the invaders took home with them a number of the sacred animals of the conquered territory. As time passed and with the harsh winter conditions of central Arabia, the cats adapted, growing longer fur. In 331BC, Persepolis, capital of Persia, was attacked by Alexander the Great. Darius, the Emperor of Persia and his court took flight into the mountains, taking with them their precious cats. North-west of what is now Meshed in eastern Persia, they would roam in the cold winter climate of the high mountains. As a result, generations of cats developed increasingly long fur. The cats also mated with local wild cats, and created the stocky build that has been associated with the Persian cat through the ages.

By 247AD the merchants of Persia had begun exporting some of the cats to neighbouring regions and by the eighth century, when Islam was flourishing, the beautiful, long-coated cats were widespread. It would be seven centuries later before they reached Angora and Anatolia, where their shape evolved into a sleeker form. Later still, in the seventeenth century, the cats were brought to the West, by the Italian poet and traveller Pietro della Valle (1586-1652), nicknamed 'the Pilgrim'.

Della Valle was a romantic, after falling in love and marrying in Baghdad, he stayed at the court of Shah Abbas for six years and travelled throughout the region. In the Persian region of Khorasan, della Valle came across 'a cat of the figure and form of our ordinary ones, but infinitely more beautiful in the lustre and colour of its coat, which is gray without any speckles and without any spots. Most of the coat is fine, lustrous and delicate like silk but it is not shaggy... The most beautiful part of the body is the tail, which is very long and all covered with fur to a length of five or six digits.' Several years later in 1626 della Valle returned to Italy with breeding stock and from there, the ancient breed was spread to the West.

Just as the cat figured in Islam, it also had a role to play in Christian tradition. It is widely assumed that Noah took cats into the ark and the legend is that the Manx cat lost its tail as it was slow in boarding. Noah became irritated and slammed the door, thereby slicing off the cat's tail. From that time on Manx cats were tail-less. In truth Manx cats may well have originated in Cornwall and from there have been taken to the Isle of Man. They were thought to have divine powers.

Manx cats were certainly in existence in 800BC and were worshipped by ancient Britons in the south-west of England. There are many legends that associate the origins of the Manx cat in Britain with cats that had been shipwrecked from the trading vessels of the Phoenicians. One of these suggests that the Manx cat originated in Japan, and was brought to Europe by the Phoenician sailors before they were established in Britain.

Manx cats are not the only tail-less cats. Other breeds with this characteristic are found in the

Balkans, in Russia, in China, as well as the Isle of Man and previously in Cornwall. Although the Manx is best known for being tail-less, it also has two other characteristics. It has an undercoat of fur and it has an especially well-rounded rump. It is this that has given rise to its nickname, a rumpy. Those people who breed Manx cats aim to produce cats with a rump as well-rounded as an orange.

The legend of Noah and the Manx cat is not the only ancient tale that has religious origins. Various superstitions also form part of Buddhist mythology. The traditional one is that if a household cat is a light-coloured one, the household will always be well-equipped with silverware, but if the house cat is dark, the owners may be fortunate enough to be well-supplied with gold.

There is a suggestion that the cat took part in various Eastern supernatural exploits, when holy men levitated. The only established Buddhist tradition is that the cat disgraced itself before being admitted to the Nirvana. All the animals, having been summoned, hurried and scurried to the sacred place, but not the cat. It made a leisurely progress and even stopped to have a cat nap. The cat was punished by being excluded from the heavenly constellations and is not represented there.

As we have already discovered cats were first carried to Britain and Northern Europe by traders from Egypt and the Middle East, where they had enjoyed a divine status from 100AD. However, the first records of them in Britain only date from 400AD. The Celts, especially the Irish and the Welsh, gave the cat a prominence not only in their legends but in their daily life. The Celtic chroniclers were conscious of a slightly mysterious and sometimes sinister aura that seemed to surround the cat.

This element is conspicuous in the story of St Brendan and the Sea Cat. In this legend the saint, while sailing, came to a small island at the centre of a strange whirlpool. When the tide receded multitudes of fish could be caught where the sea had raged. St Brendan and his companions landed, and found their way to a small stone-built church. Inside was a very frail and aged man kneeling while he said his prayers. He immediately urged them to leave, warning them that there was a sea cat about that had reached a great size as a result of all the fish it had eaten.

St Brendan and his little company hastily set sail, and spotted a huge beast with 'great eyes like vessels of glass' swimming after them. The Saint implored Christ to 'hinder the beast'. Then another beast rose from the whirlpool and the two beasts fought fiercely with each other until both sank to the depths and were seen no more. St Brendan gave thanks to God, landed back on the island and sought out the old man, and questioned him. The old man said: 'We were twelve men from the island of Ireland that came to this place seeking the place of our resurrection. Eleven be dead, and I alone remain, awaiting, O Saint of God. And when, he had received communion from St Brendan, the old man died and was buried beside his companions.

In Ireland cats were first introduced by monks in the fourth century AD and had grown in popularity to the extent that they were even included on a list of goods regarded as essential for a potential housewife. In the ninth century, illustrations of cats had been included on the illuminated manuscripts of the 'Book of Kells'.

One Celtic folk legend of the time recounts the tale of a cat and kittens born in the stable at the same time as Jesus. Mary asked all the animals for their help to put the baby Jesus to sleep but none could oblige. Then a small grey tabby kitten climbed into the manger and curled up beside the infant Jesus, upon which the child fell asleep, lulled by the kitten's gentle purring. It is said the Madonna rewarded the tabby kitten by ensuring all tabby kittens would wear the letter 'M' on their foreheads thereafter.

Another Irish cat of legend was Pangur Ban, who belonged to a learned monk living in the eighth century at the monastery at Richenau in Austria. The monk wrote a poem about Pangur Ban, drawing the similarities between his own life and that of his beloved companion. When the two of them were together, the black-habited monk and the comely white cat, each was able to practise their art. One pursued a mouse, and the other pursued a difficult phrase for his 'little book'. Pangur Ban is the first cat to be written about in the literature of the West. The tale of Pangur Ban follows on the tradition of the clerical cat set by Pope Gregory the Great (540-604) who owned a cat as his constant companion some three centuries previously.

Elsewhere in Gaelic legend cats are associated with tales of great warrior kings and heroism. Even today stories are told of one Gaelic king whose name was Carbar. Carbar, it is said, had the head of a cat and commanded great cat armies who went into battle bearing strange wild cat skins on their helmets.

In the East a fourteenth-century medieval Persian satirical legend praises a Persian cat hero in a great battle of cats and rats. The leader of the cats was like a dragon, with a chest like a shield and claws like eagles, whereas the rats were led by a brave and judicious commander. The rats had superior weapons, but the cats had claws, fangs and, above all, their intelligence.

There are different versions of the tale and there are different outcomes. In one, after the end battle the hero cat is taken prisoner and the rats celebrate, believing they are victorious. Tied to a stake with a poor rope, the Persian cat bursts his bonds 'with a claw like an eagle and the tail of a serpent', finally single-handedly slaying and defeating the rats.

Cats were prized for their valuable role as mousers and rat-catchers. In the West as far back as the tenth century, Welsh King, Howell Dha the Good, included the following law in his rulings, that is well known to all scholars of Celtic history: 'The price of a kitten before it can see is one penny. If it has caught a mouse, its value is raised to twopence, and afterwards to fourpence. If anyone should steal or slay the cat guarding the royal granary, he shall be compelled either to forfeit an ewe or as much wheat as will cover the cat when suspended by its tail.'

Statuette of the goddess Bastet.

Chapter 2

Cats as Deity in Ancient Egypt, Greece & Rome

The ancestors of the domestic cat that sits beside a family's fireside, or chases the birds in any twenty-first century garden whether in New Hampshire, Suffolk or Rome, were welcomed by the ruling families and priests of ancient Egypt into their houses and temples. Attracted by their gracefulness and detached dignity, the Egyptians not only adopted cats as honoured members of a family but in time they were attributed with supernatural powers. They were deified.

The Egyptians had a long tradition of the gods being represented on earth as animals. Anubis, the Egyptian god of the dead, had a jackal's head, while Ta-urt, the wife of Set, had the head of a hippopotamus. Several gods of ancient Egypt were depicted as cat or part-cat and were associated with the animal from the earliest dynasties. As early as the First Dynasty, Mafdet, a lynx or ocelot goddess had the role of protecting

Pharaoh's house from snakes. It was also believed by the ancients that the great Egyptian sun god Ra took the form of a cat in his nocturnal fights with the great snake demon named Apopis. The Egyptians believed that each night Apopis would lie in wait, hoping to defeat his enemy and thus prevent the dawn. But every night Ra triumphed, causing the sun to rise. Horus, son of Osiris and Isis, is portrayed with the head of a falcon and is often surrounded by images of cats.

In early Egyptian civilisation Sekhmet, a tough war-goddess cat, was held in awe and feared by the people. Around 1500BC Sekhmet was joined by Bastet, also known as Bast. Bastet sometimes had a cat's head and was sometimes all cat. Bastet was one of the most important of the Egyptian gods, a symbol of fertility and was worshipped for the protection that she provided. Together, Sekhmet and Bastet were perceived as the two faces of the sun: Sekhmet represented the devastating heat of the destructive solar power and Bastet its life-giving qualities.

As the domestic cat in Egypt became increasingly widespread and respected as both companion and hunter, Bastet began to dominate. Legend has it that Bastet fled in a temper to the desert in Nubia where she hid in the form of a lioness. The gods Onuris and Thoth, sons of Ra, were sent to bring her back and managed to persuade

Cat mummy offering, elaborately painted and wrapped.

her to return. On the way Bastet bathed in the sacred waters of Philae and her anger dissipated and she transformed into a cat. Bastet sailed down the Nile until she reached a holy place and remained there. Thereafter it was known as 'Bubastis', meaning 'City of the Cat'.

By 900BC Bastet was depicted as a domestic cat. As a goddess of fertility, Bastet was usually portrayed as a female cat surrounded by her kittens. Bubastis became an important place of pilgrimage: every year tens of thousands of people visited it, many travelling via the Nile, so that they might pay their respects to the cat goddess Bastet. Throughout the city there were many stone carvings that paid homage to Bastet.

In the temple complex the cats were treated as sacred animals by the local inhabitants and by the officials of the temple. The cats were the special responsibility of the priests who not only fed them, but arranged for their mating and encouraged them to rear their kittens within the precincts of the temple. Inevitably the fame of the temple cats spread beyond Bubastis, initially to the sacred places of Babylon, but later far and wide throughout the Mediterranean.

Superintendents, both men and women, were appointed by the city and temple to feed every kind of sacred animal. Once a person had been selected for the office, it tended to be held thereafter by their families and was handed down from generation to generation. The father of a local family would make an offering to some particular cat by shaving part or more of his children's heads. He might shave the whole head, or half, or two-thirds of it and the clippings were then weighed on scales against silver. The silver was handed to the superintendent, who in return cut up some fish and fed it to the cat.

Each spring an annual festival was held at Bubastis in honour of the cat-headed goddess. Tokens of Bastet's beneficence were widely displayed and her presence was celebrated uproariously. A rowdy element was always in evidence. According to Herodotus, writing in the fifth century BC, more wine was drunk during the festival than in the whole of the rest of the year and it was attended by some seven hundred thousand people. When the pilgrims assembled, playing flutes, singing sometimes indecorous songs, eating and drinking, dancing, indulging in boisterous jests and even more boisterous horseplay, the result was far from edifying. Some of the visitors would take boats and, paddling as near as possible to the reedy margin of the water, would bandy quips with the crowds on the shore. In this light-hearted exchange women seem to have borne a leading part.

In her heyday Bastet was an honoured deity throughout the eastern half of the Delta. The epi-centre of Bastet's cult remained at Bubastis in the district of Egypt now known as Beni-Hassan. Archaeologists exploring the site have within living memory discovered that the mound into which they delved had been known as Tell-Basta for centuries. Despite the influence of both Islam and Judaism, both of which had a hatred of graven images, reminders of the cult of Bastet have remained until the twentieth century.

Around the time of the tenth to eighth century BC all families treated the cat differently from other animals and honoured Bastet more than the Pharaohs of the Twenty-second Dynasty. They had always identified with the cat goddess. Relics of this reverence can be found in the exquisite bronze figurine in the British Museum. Bastet is represented with large, pricked up ears. Her human body is covered by a long, close-fitting garment embroidered with a reticular design and scored with perpendicular stripes. In one hand Bastet holds the sistrum, the sacred rattle used in religious rites, and in her other hand a sort of purse known as her *aegis.* Both sistrum and purse are decorated with cat-masks. At her feet sit four small kittens. Kittens often appear with or without their divine mother, the symbol of fertility, in the art of ancient Egypt.

As a goddess incarnate, Bastet's depiction as having a human body with a cat's head, as was initially the case, or as being entirely a cat depended upon the time and the place where the statue was carved as well as the current religious views. Ancient images of ordinary cats, or 'Mau', rather than sacred ones from this period are usually naturalistic. Sometimes the sculptor or artist would depict them realistically in a relaxed pose, straight from nature. In other carvings or paintings the cat is sitting erect, as they often do in real life, with their front paws close together and their tail primly curved round them. In the sculptures their eyes are inlaid with obsidian, rock crystal, lapis-lazuli, or even with gold. The ears, or even the nose, may be pierced for rings. In some instances these adornments still exist. The cats are sometimes wearing collars or necklaces and it is likely that these were personal trinkets bestowed by the cat's owner, rather than being any part of a cult offering. In other pictures the cat is portrayed devouring a fish or a duck beneath a table.

In the Cairo Museum there is a carved chair-back that depicts Queen Tiy, the wife of Amenophis III, enjoying an outing on the water in a narrow boat. She is accompanied by two young girls, one in the prow and one in the stern. The Queen's pet cat sits in the shade under her regal chair.

The oldest recorded incidence of cat mummification dates from as far back as the Twelfth Dynasty (1991-1778BC) where at Abydos seventeen cat skeletons were discovered, each with a milk dish. Later the beloved pet cat belonging to Prince Thuthmosis in the Eighteenth Dynasty (1567-1320BC) was mummified and entombed in a great stone sarcophagus. The inscriptions on the sarcophagus refer to the goddess Osiris, or Lady Cat, together with an image of roast duck on a table, to ensure she would not go hungry into the afterlife.

Scholars have identified two types of cat among surviving feline mummies. Some are of a large animal, perhaps only half-tame and resembling a lynx. It is likely that they lived among humans, but feeding themselves. There was also a smaller form, loosely classified as *felis libyca bubastis.* This type of cat became completely domesticated while maintaining its sacred nature. Archaeologists have unearthed evidence of mass burials where thousands of cats were mummified and laid to rest wearing hand-crafted and painted feline masks. Made as offerings to Bastet, it was believed that once mummified, a cat would mediate between the gods and

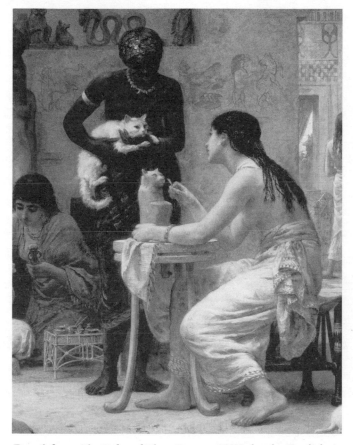

Detail from *The Gods and Their Creators*, 1878, by the English painter, Edwin Long (1829-91). Sculptures and other artistic representations of the cat were widespread in ancient Egypt.

its former owner, easing the flow of prayer and good fortune for the humans left behind. This belief became so widespread that pet cats did not always die naturally.

In a land where the cat was holy and revered and the death penalty could be applied for killing a cat, a distinctly irreverent racket arose within the priesthood. As time went on, the priests of Bastet became veritable feline factory farmers. Cats were cruelly bred and reared with the sole purpose of slaughter and embalming, to be sold to superstitious pilgrims on their visits to the temples. Cats rarely survived beyond months and only a small percentage of cat mummies reveal cats aged beyond two years. Indeed, many show that the cats have broken necks. The situation mushroomed and the extraordinary trade in mummified cats increased to industrial proportions. To fulfil demand some of the priesthood resorted to even more dubious methods, as has been proved by x-rays of some cat mummies that reveal human bones or bones of other animals, birds and reptiles, including frogs.

Herodotus, writing in the fifth century BC, told of another development that occurred within the cat population during that time. Herodotus said of the cats in Egypt that 'The number of domestic cats in Egypt is very great, and would be greater if it were not for what befalls the cats. As the females, when they have kittened, no longer seek the company of the males, these last, to obtain once more their companionship, practice a curious artifice. They seize the kittens, carry them off and kill them, but do not eat them afterwards. Upon this, the females, being deprived of their young, and longing to supply their place, seek the males once more, since they are particularly fond of their offspring.'

The mummification of cats was practised well into the Roman period. Curiously enough it was as an aid to agriculture rather than as a divine being that the Romans seem to have prized the animal. Although human mummy-powder was a popular ingredient in the Western pharmacopoeia, mummified cats were not used in the same way. However, thousands were decapitated by Arab farmers and spread upon the fields as fertilizer. One hundred and ninety of these heads were found at Gizeh. Pliny the Elder (29-79AD) notes that field-mice could be kept away from the crops if the ashes of a cat were soaked in water and then the water itself poured upon the seed. The objection to this was it made the bread taste of cat, a scientifically unlikely suggestion. Even so it encouraged the belief it was better to steep grain in ox-gall, and this avoided the problem.

The tradition of utilizing cat mummies as a crop fertilizer took a bizarre turn as recently as 1888. An

Above and opposite: Wild cats celebrating the Year of the Tiger taken from a Thai fortune telling manual, 1850, painted on folded paper.

Egyptian landowner uncovered a staggering 300,000 cat mummies, of which 80,000 were sold to Britain at £4 a ton, to be spread on fields around Liverpool to encourage the crops. Even today astonished farmers tell stories of Egyptian jewellery rising to the surface in the arable farming country of north England.

Worship of the cat goddesses had become increasingly well established over the lower reaches of the Nile and the Nile Valley during the rule of the Pharaohs and was still of importance during the Roman period. Similarly, the cat spread from ancient Egypt, where it had established an important role in everyday and temple life, to Rome, Greece and from there onwards into the rest of Europe.

As recently as the early twentieth century cats believed to be similar to the cats of ancient Egypt were recreated by Princess Natalie Troubetzkoy. In 1953, when living in Rome, the Princess noticed a pair of spotted cats owned by the Egyptian Ambassador to Italy. She had the Ambassador's tom cat, a smoke named Geppo, mated to a silver female cat named Baba that she had imported from Cairo. The Princess left Italy several years later to live in the United States, taking her cats with her. They were to form the basis of a new breed of Mau, which has grown from strength to strength. In the 1960s a breeder named Angela Sayer took up the cause of the ancient feline in the UK. Despite the Princess's preference to name the new breed the 'Egyptian Cat' the name for the breed has remained Mau, since Mau simply means 'cat' in Egyptian. The modern Mau bears a strong resemblance to those portrayed in ancient paintings.

The Greeks were not initially cat lovers and this is reflected in a dearth of references to them in Greek literature. A few poets, including Theocritus, Plutarch, Aristophanes and Timocles, referred to the cat in their writings. However, Aristotle (384-322BC), pupil of Plato and tutor of Alexander the Great, mentioned the cat only briefly. During the time that the poet spent at the court of Ptolemy Philadelphus in Alexandria he would have seen many of the cherished royal *Mau* cats. Theocritus (310-250BC), who was a Syracusan and not a Greek by birth, refers to the cat only once, in his fifth Idyll. It told of the lively colloquy between Gorgo and Praxinoë, two women of Syracuse.

It has been suggested that one of the Greek names for the cat, *ailouros*, may have been derived from two words, *ailos*, 'swift', 'changing', and *oura*, a 'tail', 'as expressive of the wavy motion of the tail peculiar to the cat-kind'. The other name was *galen*, but unfortunately

Ipuy and His Wife, fresco from the tomb of the ancient
Egyptian sculptor, Ipuy, at Deir el Medina, c.1275 BC.
In order that the deceased would feel more at home
in the afterlife, a pet cat would often feature. Here Ipuy's
kitten plays with his robe.

this is shared between the cat and the weasel, and so there is sometimes ambiguity about which is being referred to. Both beasts are sworn foes to mice, and were employed as mice-exterminators in Greece.

Despite a shortage of cat relics surviving from ancient Greece, there is some archaeological evidence to suggest the Greeks had domesticated cats. A cat is carved in a bas relief from about this time. Historians have always suggested that domesticated cats had spread to Greece and Rome from Egypt by 1000BC. They were valued both as pets and for their ability to hunt vermin. In Cyprus, a cat was found in a tomb dating from 5000BC. The cat appeared to be an African wild cat, and it is possible that this had been domesticated. In Egypt the first cats had been domesticated from about 3500BC and had become beloved pets as well as divine beings. One vase painting shows two women playing with a cat, teasing it with a bird, dating from 500BC, at the height of Etruscan culture. In around 400BC Greek coins depicted a cat, one of which was shown leaping at a bird in a woman's hand.

Romans accepted cats principally for utilitarian purposes – for its prowess in the dispatching of rodents. Cat figurines have been discovered in Roman settlements in France, Spain and in England and mosaics of cats have been unearthed at Pompeii in Italy and Orange in France. They featured in art and were carved on shields and banners. The Romans built a statue of the goddess Libertas. In one hand she bore a long rod, in the other a Phrygian cap to become, in the course of time, famous as the Cap of Liberty. At Libertas' feet sat a cat. Skeletons of cats have been discovered in domestic situations in many parts of Britain, including Kent, Chesham, Buckinghamshire, Hampshire and Monmouthshire.

The advantages of having a good mousing cat, were not without drawbacks. Two Roman writers on agriculture who flourished in the first century BC wrote of their anxiety lest their ducklings should fall prey to marauding cats. Pliny had written of the stealth that cats display when they pursue their prey and the neatness with which they devoured it. Just as today, their ancient owners sought various methods to deter them from certain objects or areas in the household. Pliny recommended putting branches of an aromatic plant known as 'rue' to keep a cat away, a method that was used well into the Middle Ages. Other deterrents were onion or vinegar, rubbed into the area that was to be protected, their acrid smell was off-putting to the sensitive nose of the cat.

In Roman literature cats were mainly ignored or

maligned. Virgil (70-19BC), the most illustrious of Roman poets, is said to have used as a theme of allusion the cat's uneasiness and the approach of rain. Ovid (43BC-17AD) hardly mentions the cat, except briefly in his *Metamorphoses*. However, some fables depicting cats attributed to both Pilpay and Aesop in 560BC, became popular throughout the Roman Empire and have been a constant theme through the ages, appearing in Greek, Latin, and in French. Some scholars dispute the existence of Aesop, since it was several centuries before *Aesop's Fables* were gathered together in one manuscript. It has been suggested that one of the fables inspired a celebrated Pompeian mosaic of a tabby at the Casa del Fauna. The cat was a particularly ferocious tabby holding captive in his claws a despairing domestic bird. The fable reads:

'The Cat, having a Mind to make a Meal of the Cock, seized him one Morning by surprise and asked him what he could say for himself why Slaughter should not pass upon him. The Cock replied that he was serviceable to Mankind by crowing in the Morning and Calling them to their daily Labour.

"That is true," says the Cat, "and is the very objection that I have against you; for you

make such a shrill, impertinent Noise that
People cannot sleep for you. Besides, you are
an incestuous Rascal who makes no Scruple
of lying with your Mother and Sisters."
"Well," says the Cock, "This I do not deny,
but I do it to procure Eggs and Chickens for
my Master." "Ah, Villain," says the Cat.
"Hold your wicked Tongue. Such Impieties as
these declare that you are no longer fit to live.'"

Another of Aesop's fables tells of a house infested with
mice and of the successful efforts of a cat in managing
their numbers. 'The mice in council resolved that none
of them should descend from the topmost shelf.' Over
two thousand years later, these ancient moral tales
depicting animals with human characteristics enjoyed a
renaissance, when the seventeenth-century writer Jean
de la Fontaine (1621-1695) polished and extended
Aesop's original tales in a collection of 230 fables.

Some four centuries later Sicilian Greek historian
Diodorus Siculus (90-21BC) was no less impressed by
the cult of cat worship. With an amused eye he watched
the Egyptians crumbling bread into milk or cutting up
fish for the cats that they would summon to the
banquet 'with a clucking sound'. He had observed that

The Cat's Paw, illustration by Charles H Bennett (1828-1867) from *The Fables of Aesop and Others* published 1857.

if anyone killed an ibis or a cat they were in danger of being lynched by the mob. As a result, should anyone notice a cat lying dead he or she would run away as fast as possible.

Nevertheless, both Greeks and Romans identified the cat with Artemis or Diana. 'When the gods', wrote Ovid, 'fled into Egypt and hid themselves there under borrowed forms, the sister of Apollo appeared in the guise of a cat.' He does not say that she wore the head of a cat as would have been the case had it been an Egyptian cat god. To the Jewish prophets the worship of the cat in graven images was repugnant. The tendency of their people to 'go a-whoring after strange gods' must have lent a sharper edge to their fury.

In the early Christianity, the worship of the cat was greeted with equal disdain. Despite this, a few early saints were known to have adored their feline companions, including St Gregory the Great (540-504). Gregory began as a Roman civil servant but gave up worldly life to live in a monastery with his cat as his only companion. Jacobus Diaconus wrote that Gregory would carry the cat on his chest, frequently stroking it. Soon afterwards he rose stratospherically through the ranks of the Church to become Pope. One version of the story of Pope Gregory and his cats recounts that it was not Pope

Gregory but a hermit whose only possession was a cat. The hermit was told in a dream he would 'be in the same place as Pope Gregory' and through the re-telling of the story the cat's ownership became confused over time.

Cat and rat, taken from a thirteenth century edition of the
Panchatanva, an ancient Indian collection of animal fables.

Chapter 3

MEDIEVAL CATS
OF LORE & LEGEND

The cat had been legendary in Egypt and featured heavily in mythology. In both its original home in the Middle East and in Northern Europe its prowess as a rat and mouse slayer also commended it to its owners on a practical level.

In the East the great Muslim warrior El Daher Beybars, Sultan of Egypt and Syria in the thirteenth century, was reputed to be as kind to cats as he was brave and fearsome on the battlefield. He is said to have bequeathed a beautiful garden named Gheyt al Quottah (the cat's orchard) to help support strays. The garden was near the mosque dedicated to his name in Cairo and although the mosque subsequently fell into ruin and the orchard was lost, the tradition of cat feeding in the area was held up for centuries thereafter.

Cats, as hunters of rats and mice, were in demand and spread rapidly through the towns and villages of

Britain. Although their ability to protect corn from vermin was useful, they never integrated into families as easily as dogs. The mystery and apparent detachment of the cat put it apart from other animals, so that it once again achieved a near-mythical status. It wasn't to last.

The cat was persecuted. Superstitions about cats grew, they were thought to have a sinister, devilish connection. Dante (1265-1321) wrote of cats in his poetry only once, comparing them to demons who, with their hooked claws, claw the barterers when these sinners try to emerge from the hot pitch in which they are being punished. He says of one of these 'among wicked cats came the mouse'.

Another sinister image of the cat is evident in the French church at Canterbury. A cat forms part of the capital of a column, but the cat is not the sort that would be a welcome companion. Its tale is bifurcated and each branch ends in a snake's head.

Even at the time when they were being most persecuted, there were still those who loved their cats, but they were in a minority. The average twelfth-century Britain was liable to throw a stone, or worse, at any cat on his or her premises. During this period, hundreds of thousands of cats were cruelly slaughtered. They were hung, burnt and often horribly tortured before being killed. The population of European cats that had become firmly established following their introduction from the Middle East was reduced to a tenth of what it had been before superstitions had grown up about them.

Several hundred years after Westminster Abbey was built, reconstruction of one of its earliest sections revealed that a cat had been walled up in a cavity in the building at the time when the foundations were laid. The spirit of the cat was thought to keep evil at bay and the tradition of placing cats in the walls of new houses as a way of supposedly protecting the buildings against rats and mice continued until as late as the eighteenth century.

Numerous incidences of these 'vermin-scares' dating have been discovered not only in walls, but also under floorboards or doorsteps, often with a mouse or rat ceremoniously placed in the mouth of the cat. Several cats have been unearthed as recently as the 1950s in areas of London such as Southwark and Bloomsbury, as well as in the Tower of London. Inspection of a medieval cottage in Essex revealed a cat and her kittens plastered into a wall and there are examples in Cambridge and in Dublin where a cat was found buried behind the organ in Christchurch

Cathedral. Elsewhere in Europe the practice of walling up cats into houses was equally commonplace. In recent times a cat was even found in an old charnel house in Rouen, and there have been others discovered in Gibraltar and in Sweden.

Just as there were some surfs and ordinary villagers who treasured their cats, so there was an association between the cat and those who led a religious life. During the reign of Philip IV, Philippe le Bel, of France (1285-1314), the Knights Templar, a mystical, part Christian, part Luciferian order, were suppressed and their lands were confiscated. Their opponents, whose opinion may have been motivated by jealousy for their great wealth, claimed that Satan himself was apt to appear at their midnight services. The devil appeared in the form of a large black tom cat. The enemies of the Templars, anxious to discredit them, claimed that children were sacrificed to keep the fiendish creature on side. The Templars were thought to have been linked to freemasonry. One theory is that freemasonry itself owed some of its origins to ancient Egyptian beliefs and the worship of the goddess Isis. Isis was associated with Bastet, the cat goddess.

Other religious circles had a softer opinion of the cat and it was even associated with various female saints, including St Martha, thought by some to have been responsible for the cat's welfare, as was St Gertrude of Nivelles, Patron Saint of cats and gardeners. St Agatha is also known as the 'Santo Gato' (Cat Saint), in south western France. According to local legend, St Agatha appeared as an enraged cat to women who did not rest from their work on 5th February, the saint's feast day in France.

The long affinity between women and cats holds true as much within the ecclesiastical community as later, in the association between witches and their familiars. In the thirteenth century a kindly, cat-loving ecclesiastic drew up the *Ancren Riwle*, an anchoress's code, for the guidance of a small Cistercian community of holy women. Although the women were recluses, the Church authorities understood human nature all too well to deprive them completely of every outlet for their natural affections.

The code suggests that sisters need not wear hair-shirts, walk barefoot, beat themselves with holly and briars or subsist on pulses and water. Milk was allowed in their diet, and the anchoress was allowed to keep a cat with whom she could share the contents of her bowl. They were, however, only allowed one cat. 'Ye, mine leove sustren,' says the Rule, 'ne schulen

The examinacion

sayde Catte with breade and mylke and she dyd so, also she taughte her to cal it by the name of Sathan and to kepe it in a basket.

When this mother Eue had geuen her the Cat Sathan, then this Elizabeth desired firste of the sayde Cat (callinge it Sathan) that she might be ryche and to haue goodes, and he promised her she shoulde, askinge her what she would haue, and she sayde shepe(for this Cat spake to her as she confessed in a straunge holowe boice, (but suche as she vnderstode by vse) & this Cat forthwith brought shepe into her pasture to the nüber of.xviii blacke haben no Best bute Kat one' (Ye, my dear sisters, shall have no beast but one cat). The cat kept the nuns' cells free from rats and mice, but it was also a companion during the long hours when its mistress was alone and had no human contact. The church authorities never objected to the occasional cat kept in the cloisters. Whereas dogs, monkeys, even tame rabbits, might disturb the life of the community, a cat could be trusted to behave with a decorum that wouldn't be distracting.

Cat's fur was used to trim a woman's dress, especially those designed for nuns. At this time the type of dress a woman could wear was determined by her husband's social status, rather than his income. Miniver and marten, gryse and vair were the prerogative of those of royal and noble rank, but lamb, cat and rabbit-skin provided the fur that could be worn by those of the lower classes. Cat's fur was for some reason regarded as especially suitable for nuns. Desiderius Erasmus (1465-1536), the Dutch scholar and philosopher, visited England in 1498 remarking that the earls there were wearing cloaks trimmed with

Opposite: A sixteenth century woodcut illustrates perfectly the Medieval association of the cat with the devil.

cat fur. In a letter to a friend he mentions that a visit to an English home required not only kissing the host and hostess and their children, but also the family cat.

Nuns weren't the only religious people who valued their cats. Bartholomew, a Friar Minor and a follower of the greatest of animal lovers, St Francis, also wrote about cats. Although the Franciscans didn't always live in monasteries because much of their time was spent as travelling preachers, they had houses where they stayed between their journeys. Bartholomew, an Englishman, wrote of the cat in his encyclopaedic work, *De Natura Rerum*, and has many things to say that are as relevant today as they were in the thirteenth century. 'The cat is in youth', he tells us, 'a full lecherous beast. He is swift, pliant and merry, he leapeth and climbeth on everything that is before him; he is led by a straw and playeth therewith, and is a right heavy beast in age, and full sleepy, and lieth slyly in wait for mice, and is aware where they be more by smell than by sight, and hunteth and pounceth upon them in privy places. And when he taketh a mouse he playeth therewith and eateth him after the play.' Unlike the nuns and some other more senior monks, friars wore no fur, not even catskin, on their habits.

In the thirteenth century an international disaster

ensured the cat's utilitarian role again became of prime importance to the ordinary working people as well as those in religious orders. European traders, and quite possibly returning crusaders, inadvertently brought back to their homelands a different breed of rats that was stronger and more adaptable than previously. The black rats carried the bubonic plague, or Black Death, that devastated Europe during the fourteenth century. Cats, whose popularity had been waning, were suddenly again in demand. They were no longer persecuted and were allowed to multiply. The more they multiplied, the greater the number of rats and mice that were killed and the number of people who died from the plague was reduced. The cat's status was restored.

During this period, Francesco Petrarch (1304-1374), Italian poet and scholar, was among those who held a high esteem and fondness for cats and in particular his own pet. The historian Louise Caldi writes that Petrarch's chief companion was his cat. When the poet died, the cat was put to death and embalmed. Today the cat's mummified body lies in a niche adorned with a marble cat at Petrarch's home, Arquá, in the Euganean Hills in Italy, bearing a Latin inscription that translates as 'I was the greatest passion, second only to Laura'. Tragically Laura, the only rival for the poet's affection, died of the plague only a year after meeting him.

It wasn't only on land that the cats had proved their worth as mousers. Since Egyptian times they had demonstrated they kept the rat numbers on board ship down. Cats became established members of the crew on both merchant and naval vessels. Just as those who lived on the land had mixed views about cats, so did seafarers. A wealth of superstition grew about the seafaring felines. Sailors were always, and still are, in two minds about having animals aboard. They welcomed their presence but to talk about them, or even to refer about animals that they had left behind on shore, was, and remains today, unlucky.

Fishermen may blame talk of animals for a poor catch, sailors for a bad storm and seafaring traders for an unprofitable trip. It was especially unlucky to say the word 'pat' while onboard. The origin of this superstition is thought to stem from its similarity of the use of the word 'cat' in 'cat o nine tails', rather than to the animal.

In some seafaring cultures the cat had a mystical power as well as a rat-catching prowess. Japanese sailors were convinced that having a tortoiseshell cat that would climb up the rigging to the top of the mast was a sure way of driving storm devils away.

Cats featured in literature as well as in legends of the period, in the East as well as the West. In Persia in the fourteenth century Obaid-e Zakani wrote a tale for children entitled *Cat and Mouse* that is still told today. The story tells of the cat Tibbald who goes to pray forgiveness for killing and eating a mouse. To make amends he offers a token gift of compensation to the surviving relatives of the mouse who, delighted, rush to see him. But Tibbald, the betrayer, turns on them and eats all but two of the mice, who manage to escape. The king of the mice vows to avenge their deaths and war breaks out between the cats and mice. Tibbald is captured but finally escapes, after he has eaten the Lord Chief Justice.

Chaucer (1328–1400) gives a good description of cats in his *Canterbury Tales*, stressing their beauty and the sleekness of their fur.

'For whoso wolde sege a cattes skyn,
Thenne wolde the cat wel dwellen in hir in;
And is the cattes skyn be slyk and gay,
She wol nat dwelle in house half a day.
But forth she wol, er any day be dawed,
To shewe hir skyn, a goon a-caterwawed.'

In 'The Miller's Tale', Robyn, the young servant of the Oxford carpenter, stooped and peered through a hole in the door 'Ful low upon a bord, Ther as the cat was wont in for to crepe.' Although this cat had to creep through the hole in the door to find a comfortable bed, this was not always necessary. In both The Manciple's Tale and that of the 'Wife of Bath', cats figure. In the 'Manciple's Tale' advice is given as to how to feed and look after a cat. He stresses a comfortable bed of silk.

> 'Let take a cat, and foster hire with milk
> And tendre flesh, and make hire couche of silke,
> And let hir see a mous go by the wall,
> Anon she weiveth milke and flesh, and all,
> And every deintee that is in that house,
> Swiche appetit hath she to ete the mous.'

The 'Wife of Bath' describes the habits of cats and is especially interested in the behaviour of female cats rather than the male.

Other tales and fables during the troubled reign of Richard II, both in England and in Scotland recount the stories of mice or rats who wanted to hang a bell around the neck of their arch-enemy, the cat. These stories were popular because the cat became the symbol of the oppressive and extortionate ruling classes and the rats and mice in the tales represented the downtrodden peasants. It was from a Scottish tale about James III in which Archibald Douglas, the Earl of Angus, is said to have coined the phrase 'to bell a cat'. This is still in use today.

However much the cat was reviled, its usefulness as a predator against rodents was acknowledged. In the fifteenth century the value of a cat as a protector of homes and crops against mice was recognized in the codes and customs of various European countries.

This fifteenth-century German woodcut depicts the words of the proverb 'Beware of those cats that lick from the front and claw from behind'.

On one occasion King Louis XI was out hunting with harriers at Montlouis, between Tours and Amboise, when his hounds fell upon and killed the cat of a poor cottage woman. Though not the most open-handed of monarchs, he gave the good dame a crown – the same sum that would have been indicated if the victim had been a goose or a sheep.

Across the channel Britain's Cardinal Wolsey (1471-1530), advisor to Henry VIII, was a great lover of cats and would take his own pets to important meetings, state dinners and even to church services. Wolsey was known to conduct his business as Chancellor of England with his favourite black cat beside him on his throne.

The heralds of medieval England preferred dogs to cats as crests and supporters in coats of arms. Those who carried out the same role north of the Border used the cat in some coats of arms, but not the domestic cat, rather the Scottish wild cat. The cat *sejeant gardant proper* of the Grants of Ballindalloch is no 'Jolly Gib' but a real cat-a-mountain; hence, no doubt, the warning motto, *Touch not the cat but a glove*. The Macintosh clan of Caithness, who were the descendants of the Catti or Clan Chattan, bore the same motto, and had two cats *salient gardant proper* as their supporters. The ducal house

Detail of horseman with panther owned by Giovanni de Medici, taken from the *Adoration of the Angels and the Three Magi* by Benozzo de Lesse (c.1421-1497).

of Sutherland also bears a cat-a-mountain *salient*.

One tradition has it that the family owes its descent through the female line from a Northern invader who, on landing at Littleferry, about four miles from Dunrobin, was pounced upon by a number of ferocious wild cats. The fight that ensued was fierce and long, but in the end all the cats were slain, and the courageous invader became the first Thane of Sutherland.

The most celebrated cat in heraldry was probably one that existed only in the jangling imagination of Don Quixote de la Mancha. Among the knights whom he believed that he beheld when he came upon a peacefully grazing flock of sheep was a certain Timonel de Carcajona, Prince of New Biscay, whose shield bore the figure of a cat, and the laconic motto, 'Miau'.

Artists of the medieval period, like the heralds, usually preferred to paint dogs rather cats. Every type of dog is shown in pictures of the time, while cats must have held themselves characteristically aloof.

Opposite: Title page of *Aristotelis Naturalis*, Venice, 1546, depicting a cat with its prey in its mouth. The great Greek author Aristotle mentions the cat only briefly in his writings but during the Middle Ages the cat's value as a mouser enjoyed a renaissance.

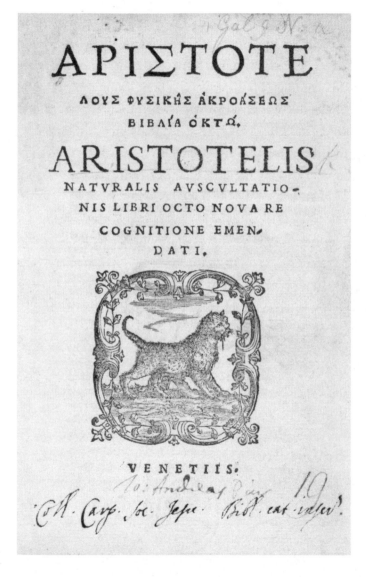

However, Pinturicchio painted a classic tabby in his picture of the *Return of Ulysses*. In Tintoretto's picture of Christ washing the Disciple's feet a dusky cat looks on aloofly. The cat is so dark in colour and so unobtrusive that it is only noticed when the painting is studied carefully. For Leonardo da Vinci (1452-1519), however, 'even the smallest feline is a work of art'. He showed his liking for the animal by making numerous cat drawings and studies during this period. In contrast to the crucial utilitarian and practical role of the cat during the Middle Ages, its association with all things supernatural continued to grow. Early Egyptian reverence had subsided, giving way to an increasing mistrust and in some quarters a fear of the feline species. The animal once linked to the gods and then with the devil led to a gamut of superstitions and sayings, many of which have survived to the present day.

Pregnant women were the object of two entirely contradictory superstitions. In Eastern Europe it was believed that a cat would increase the chances of fertility of a young couple. A month after the wedding a special fertility ceremony took place in which a cat would be secured in a cradle and was carried to the couple's house where it was rocked from side to side like a baby. Elsewhere, if a pregnant woman was in pain, it was believed she was bewitched and there were kittens scratching at her inside. Any woman believing herself to be cursed and about to give birth to kittens would understandably become agitated. This led to the common expression of someone 'having kittens' and for centuries having an abortion was often referred to as releasing the kittens in the belly.

Other sayings were less to do with superstition than by association of an object or a situation. Nowadays we say 'there's no room to swing a cat'. The 'cat' refers to a whip named 'the cat' that was used on sailing ships to punish errant sailors, so called on account of the claw-like wounds it carved on sailors' backs. Later, the

Above left: Drawing of a cat by Michelangelo (1475-1564).

Above right: Study of a cat by Leonardo da Vinci (1452-1519).

phrase 'letting the cat out of the bag' was coined when tradesmen would take piglets to market in a bag ready to be sold. Sometimes the men would put a cat instead of the pig in the bag, pretending it was a pig. If the cat escaped, the trick would be exposed and hence the saying. The bag, often called a poke, also gave rise to the saying 'never buy a pig in a poke'.

Cats also played a part in the local folklore and medieval miracle plays. Among the liveliest of the latter was that of the *Deluge*, acted by the Waterdrawers of Chester. As the animals, represented by 'cut-outs', were hustled aboard the Ark, Noah's three sons, with some assistance from their wives, called out the names of the cats and dogs.

The legend of the cat who by ridding an Oriental potentate's palace of rats and mice won a fortune for her lucky owner is found in many European folk tales. In England it has always been famously associated with the name of Dick Whittington.

Dick Whittington was born in the 1350s, the youngest son of a Gloucestershire squire, who came to London and made a fortune from trading in expensive textiles, supplying velvets and silks to the aristocracy. He may well have had a cat, but it is thought that the phrase 'Dick Whittington and his cat' in fact stemmed

An engraving from 1876 depicts the merchant and politician Richard Whittington and his cat, the real life inspiration for the folk tale Dick Whittington and his Cat.

from the name of the ships in which the fabric was brought to London. These were known as 'cata'.

The story of Dick Whittington's wealth has, over the years, been combined with the tale of the mouse-ridden palace of the King of Barbary. The legend was that Dick Whittington's master was appalled by the plague of mice from which the King of Barbary was suffering and immediately offered Whittington and his cat as the remedy. The cat was an efficient mouser and rid the palace of the infestation. Dick was then placed in a quandary because the King wanted to buy the cat for a great price. Dick was torn between the love of his cat and his desire to serve his master, as well as the strong urge to make a small fortune. His trading instincts triumphed and his cat was left behind.

A simpler version of the legend is that Dick Whittington's cat was a mouser loaned to a ship before it set sail on a trading voyage. The cat cleared the ship of a plague of rats and earnt Dick a fortune.

It is beyond doubt that Whittington, the squire's son from Gloucestershire, went on to become the Lord Mayor of London three times in the late fourteenth and early fifteenth centuries, from 1397 to 1399, 1406 to 1407 and 1419 to 1420. In 1416 he also became MP for the city of London and according to some scholars married Alice, daughter of Sir Ivo Fitzwaryn. They had no children.

It is also recorded that his business was so successful that he was rich enough to loan large sums of money to both King Henry IV and Henry V. On his death in 1423 he bequeathed a fortune to charity. Just as versions of the tale of Dick Whittington have been polished and embellished down the ages, with pedlars hawking it about the country in uncouth prose and even more uncouth verse, there has been much argument concerning his cat. There is solid evidence that about the time Dick Whittington was Lord Mayor, there was a very special cat in London. The various myths of the cat have been told by children's nurses to their charges as they sat round the fire. Even Pepys describes one version he had seen in a puppet-show at Southwark Fair. He found it 'pretty to see'.

In 1862 workmen found evidence to support the story that Dick owned a beloved cat. The workmen were digging near the site of a house in Gloucester, traditionally associated with the Whittington family, when they unearthed a small carving of a boy holding something that looked uncommonly like a cat.

Abortive efforts have been made over the centuries to find the grave of Whittington. During the Second

World War, the Church of St Michael Paternoster Royal, designed by Wren and occupying the site next door to where Dick Whittington was said to have lived, was wrecked by a bomb. The church was built on the site of an earlier fifteenth-century church. There was a legend that gold treasure had been buried in the coffin of Dick Whittington in the earlier church. In the reign of Edward VI a parson broke it open, and only in the following reign of Mary I did the parishioners reopen the vault. They found the wizened body of a cat. Although there was a memorial to the cat, it couldn't possibly have been contemporary with Dick Whittington.

Opposite: The legend of Dick Whittington and his cat passed into folklore through the spoken word and theatre. Many versions of the tale were also recorded in print from the Middle Ages onwards. This illustration, taken from one edition dated 1845 entitled *Whittington and his cat* by one Sir R Whittington shows Dick handing over his cat to the captain of a ship.

he delivered her to the captain; "for now," said Dick, "I shall be kept awake again all night by the rats and mice."

Those who were present, laughed at Dick's strange article for adventure: but Miss Alice, who felt pity for the poor boy, gave him some half-pence to buy another cat.

This and many other instances of kindness

In traditional folklore witches have always been accompanied by a faithful black cat companion.

Chapter 4

DEVILLISH CATS & CENTURIES OF PERSECUTION

The association of cats with witchcraft dates back as far as the tenth century, when in the year 962 each Wednesday during Lent, hundreds of cats were burned in the belief that they were witches in disguise. So began a reign of cruel persecution that was to continue for centuries.

There was a brief period of respite for the poor cat following the Crusades in the thirteenth century. The ships carrying the returning Crusaders also transported the Black Rat, which carried the deadly Bubonic plague into the heart of the city of London. Cats became in demand to control the scourge, but the reign of terror for witches and their cats continued and worsened during the fifteenth century.

In the sixteenth and seventeenth centuries Christian persecutions ensured 100,000 witches were executed in Germany, 75,000 in France and 30,000 in Britain, along with hundreds of thousands of cats. As late as 1658 Edward Topsell, in his authoritative work of natural history, wrote that 'the familiars of Witches do most ordinary appear in the shape of Cats, which is an argument that this beast is dangerous to soul and body'. William Shakespeare's attitude to cats, and even poet Sir Philip Sidney's passing reference to ugly and unlucky cats shows that by the sixteenth century the cat had an evil reputation.

Some scholars argue that the origins of the supposed association of cats with witchcraft stretch still further back into the mists of time. Even some Romans describing cats used terms that could mean, and had meant originally, something dedicated, holy and set apart. But later *sacer*, the word used, from which

Drawing of a domestic cat taken from Edward Topsell's *Natural History of Four Footed Beasts*, 1658.

we derive the word 'sacred', could also refer to something that was wicked and horrible. This word spans the divide between Bastet, the beneficent cat-headed goddess, and the Graymalkin, the cat-shaped familiar spirit, to whom the First Witch in *Macbeth* exclaims 'I come'.

Exactly why the cat became the object of such vilification and cruelty has been the subject of much speculation. Some have argued that it was a reaction against the cat's ancient sacred symbolism, and its connection with childless, elderly women during the medieval period. Other theories draw on the connection between caterwauling during the breeding season and its association with orgies and secret magical ceremonies.

In medieval Europe the cat lost the revered and sacred status it had enjoyed in Ancient Egypt and was now seen as wicked and linked directly with the devil. Freya, the Viking goddess of love became an evil witch and her faithful cats were loathed as witches' familiars. It was widely believed that kittens selected to be witches' familiars were suckled by the witch.

Long before the Reformation nuns welcomed cats as their companions. After it the association of cats with usually childless, single, old women, who were no

In Viking mythology the goddess Freya rode in a chariot pulled by two black or grey cats.

longer part of a religious order may have been the origin of the concept of witches and their cats. By then, and possibly even before, a solitary old woman, whether widow or spinster, around whose lonely hearth a black cat sat purring was inevitably regarded as a witch. If her cat innocently and in a gesture of friendly welcome came out to greet its mistress, tail in air, suspicion fell even more cruelly upon each of them. The apparent offence would have been compounded if the cat had thrust its head into the old woman's hand before she hobbled back to her cottage with an armful of sticks.

While Cambridge dons, courtiers and literary figures were tolerant of their own cats, who enjoyed a comfortable and well-fed life, society wasn't so kind to the cat of the witch. The cat was not seen in the same light as the cossetted household moggy. The witch's cat was a familiar and was assumed to have as many, if not more, supernatural powers than its mistress. The witch's cat was also usually depicted as being black. Its very presence caused anxiety and there was always suspicion that in some sinister way it might get even with anyone who taunted or mocked it. That they were not all black is indicated by the name of one witch's cat that figured in an indictment, as a 'white kitling'.

Black cats were often singled out for the cruelest treatment as they were considered to be the most wicked. It is said that the devil would borrow the coat of a black cat when he wished to torture his prey. As a result, all-black cats became less common, while those black cats with even a small amount of white fur survived and even today most black cats have a slight patch of white somewhere. The modern superstition that it is lucky for a black cat to cross your path derives directly from the idea that evil has passed you by, and so you have survived the bad luck it brought. In North America the opposite meaning applies. It is considered bad luck for a black cat to cross your path and is derived directly from the original superstition of the black cat as the harbinger of evil and misfortune.

One black cat considered to be particularly evil was Rutterkin, the familiar belonging to the seventeenth-century English servant of the Earl of Rutland, Joan Flower, who was accused of being a witch. Rutterkin was said to have evil eyes like burning coal. Joan and her two daughters were believed to have been aided by Rutterkin in their 'evil influence' on the Rutland family. Both sons of the Earl had died and his wife had become barren. Joan's daughters were hanged in 1617 and Joan, protesting her innocence, choked while eating in prison and died before she could suffer the same fate. It remains a mystery what happened to Rutterkin, though it is unlikely he survived.

Grey-coloured cats were also thought to be wicked. In 1969 Brian Vesey-Fitzgerald wrote that 'the true cat of witchcraft, the true familiar of the witch, was the grey cat, Grimalkin'. The well-known seventeenth-century term 'grimalkin', meaning 'cat', and in particular an old female one, had originally been

Detail of cat cleaning his face with his paw taken from *Joseph in Prison,* by an unidentified Flemish painter known as the Master of the Story of Joseph (c.1500). The menacing expression here is very different to more benign images seen in many contemporary paintings.

coined as a result of the association between cats and woman. Gradually, 'Grimalkin' came to refer not just to a cat, but to a jealous old woman and later to mean an enemy resembling a grey cat. Desmond Morris describes the derivation of the word 'Grimalkin' as follows: 'Grimalkin = Grey + Malkin. Malin = Maud + kin. Maud = abbreviation of Matilda. Matilda = slang term for a slut'.

White cats were similarly persecuted, despite one benevolent folk tale of the White Cat, based on an ancient fable by Aesop. This story left a more positive, endearing image of the cat. In 1682 the Comtesse D'Aulnoy wrote a version in which a handsome prince falls in love with a beautiful white cat and wants to marry her. She asks that he cut off her head and her tail and throw them in the fire. With great reluctance, he agrees, upon which she is freed from an ancient curse and is turned back into the beautiful princess she really was. They live happily ever after.

This tale was the exception. The rule was that all varieties and colours of cats were cruelly tortured and put to death during the witch-hunting ages. Today, nobody with any degree of sensitivity would tolerate the barbarities then practised upon cats and other animals. But during this period many onlookers enjoyed it all prodigiously.

As cats were considered to be endowed with supernatural powers, to help in the practice of black magic and to be in league with witches and the devil, they were tortured and sacrificed. The Church supported these activities and on feast days the saints were celebrated by burning large numbers of cats alive as part of the festivities.

Cruelty to cats had become accepted as a form of public entertainment. One horrid spectacle was that of the very popular cat organ, an instrument designed to make music out of the cries of a group of terrified cats. It is recorded that one such instrument of torture was paraded through the streets of Brussels in 1549 in honour of King Philip II. A bear sat playing the cat organ, which contained some twenty cats, confined in narrow boxes, their tails sticking out of the top and tied to ropes that were in turn attached to the organ keys. When the keys were pressed the cords tightened and the tails were pulled, causing the unfortunate cats to meow. Other versions of the instrument contained spikes instead of ropes, which stuck into the poor cats. Such cruel torture remained fashionable for another century until it finally faded out and was replaced by curious forms of cat singing and cat operas in the Georgian age.

King James VI of Scotland and James I of England regarded himself an expert on magic and witchcraft. His credulity and obstinacy now seem unspeakably cruel and in no way more so than when dealing with witches. His attitude only reflected the spirit of the times. Pope Innocent VIII had written the *Malleus Maleficarum*, the 'Hammer for Witches' in the late fifteenth century. In the opinion of King James and the Church this left no doubt about the theory that the devil's disciples were able to turn themselves into animals, especially cats.

King James does not specifically allude to a familiar spirit in the form of a cat. However, during the many trials for witchcraft at which he presided, he must have regularly heard more than enough about these so-called four-footed servants of Satan. Agnes Thompson of Haddinton, 'the eldest witch of them all', in her confession gave the King cause to disapprove of reputed witches, leading him to believe that a cat was frequently involved in their heathen practices.

Having startled the King by repeating to him the very words which passed between him and the Queen

Opposite: The Love Potion, by Evelyn de Morgan (1850-1919) features a witch accompanied by her familiar, a black cat. Familiars were regarded as servants of the devil.

on their wedding-night at Oslo in Norway, the crone admitted that by her arts she had raised the storms which delayed the sailing of the King's ship. Agnes Thompson had confessed to having caused the storm 'at his cumming foorth of Denmark' that had also sunk another ship, which was sailing to Leith. The ship was carrying a cargo of 'sundrye Jewells and riche gifts' that were to have been presented to the Queen on her return to Scotland. The method adopted by Agnes to bring about the catastrophe was as cruel as the process of 'swimming a witch', with its inevitable end – death. In her confession she describes the technique she used to summon the storm. She 'took a Cat and christened it, and afterwards bound to each part of that Cat the chiefest parts of a dead man and several joints of his body, and that in the night following the said Cat was conveyed into the midst of the sea by all these witches sailing in their riddles or sieves as aforesaid, and so left the said Cat right before the Towne of Leith in Scotland. This done there did arise such a Tempest in the Sea as greater hath not been seen.'

Agnes Thompson was not the only Scottish witch who was, in the minds of her accusers, devilishly involved with cats. In 1596 a sisterhood of witches in Aberdeen were said to have turned themselves into cats and in this transformation enjoyed orgies around the cross in the centre of the fish market. A possible explanation that accounts for an apparent magical change from witch to cat is that Scottish witches of the time wore mantels and veils of fur and masks bearing cat features, in which they danced.

Shakespeare's contemporaries also brought witches and cats into their plays. Very often, as in Thomas Heywood's *The Witches of Lancashire*, cats and witches could swap personalities and one could become incarnate in the other. Heywood (1574–1641) takes us to a haunted mill, and brings upon the scene a Miller with scratched and bloody hands. 'Cats do you call them?' exclaims the victim,

> 'for their hugeness they might be cat-a-mountains. Good landlord, provide yourself with a new tenant. I'll not endure such another night if you would give me your Mill for nothing.'

A stout-hearted soldier volunteers to take over the mill; but he, too, has a disturbed night, harassed by the witches. When he 'stops their caterwauling with his bilbo' and cuts off what he took to be a cat's paw, he finds that it is the hand of Mrs Generous, a witch.

Thomas Middleton (1518-1627) wrote *The Witch* between 1609 and 1616, but it wasn't published until 1778. Although scholars disagree about the influence of *Macbeth* on *The Witch*, no one disputes that there are more cats in Middleton's works than in Shakespeare's. In *The Witch* one of the familiars is named 'Kit-with-the-Candlestick'; a spirit in the form of a cat who descends to demand her dues – a kiss and a sip of blood. The sisterhood of witches then flew away over steeples, turrets and towers.

'The Cat sings a brave treble in her own language', commented Firebrace, the Witch's son; and later in the play he remarked, 'I know as well as can be when my Mother's mad and our great cat angry, for one spits French then, and the other spits Latin.'

It was not necessary to christen a cat profanely or to drown it in order to whip up a storm. There was an implicit understanding that powers of this sort were held by all witches. Sometimes they would exercise it when annoyed, from which it seems to follow that Graymalkin might on occasion help out to oblige friends.

The notorious Matthew Hopkins had been appointed the first official Witch Finder General of England in 1644. He travelled the country in this role and was described as sending hundreds of hapless old women to their death. Many were mentally disturbed, others were intellectuals who refused either to submit to the will of the mob or abandon their principles. Once designated a witch they were doomed and so were their four-footed companions.

Not all witches' familiars were cats, in many cases they were more likely to have been animals derived from the imagination of the prosecution. In the frontispiece to Hopkins' *Discovery of Witches* (1647) five

Illustration showing two witches and the names of their familiars from Matthew Hopkins '*Discovery of Witches*', 1647

familiars are portrayed in attendance on two witches. Of these five, two are fantastic beasts, one is a black hare named 'Sacke and Sugar', one a rat-like creature called 'Newes', and only one that is unmistakably a cat. Perhaps it is a kitten. The witch stretches her hand towards it, and it approaches her with confidence, tail in the air, when she addresses it as 'Holt'. Matthew Hopkins stands in the background, watching them narrowly. Poor Holt by showing so plainly that he was on such good terms with his mistress may have sealed her fate – and his own.

Although witches received such little justice, not everybody was taken in by it. 'Every old woman.' says John Gaule, a Puritan parson of the time, 'with a wrinkled face, a hairy lip, a squint eye, a spindle in her hand, and a dog or cat by her side, is not only suspected but pronounced for a witch.'

Calvinistic preoccupation with witchcraft crossed the Atlantic in the company of the Pilgrim Fathers, coloured their ideas, darkened their judgement, and resulted in the notorious Witch-Hunts at Salem, Massachusetts in 1692. One hundred and fifty people stood accused, of which fifty were acquitted, thirteen were hanged, one crushed to death and one died naturally. Those set free were saved by the testimony of a man named Robert Downer who, giving evidence against Susanna Martin, told the hearing that she had told him that a 'she-devil' would 'fetch him away'. Shortly afterwards a cat came in through his window and, he said, grabbed him by the throat, upon which he invoked the Holy Trinity. It is said that the cat quickly ran away and took flight out of the window.

Richard Chamberlayn, a young gentleman of Gray's Inn, was staying in the house of a planter named George Walter, in New Hampshire. His stay coincided with an incidence of what he learnedly describes as *Lithobolia*, or the 'throwing of stones' at cats associated with witchcraft.

> 'In the Evening, as soon as I had supped in the outer room before mine, I took a little Musical Instrument and began to touch it (the door indeed was set open for Air) and a good big stone came rumbling in and as it were to lead the dance, but upon a much different Account than in days of Old and of old, fabulous Enchantments, my Musick being none of the best. The Noise of this brought up the Deputy-President's Wife and many others of the neighbourhood who were

below, who wondered to see this Stone
followed, as it were, by many others and a
Pewter Spoon among the rest ... And beside
all this there was seen by two Youths in the
Orchard and Fields, as they said, a black Cat
at the time the Stones were tossed about, and
it was shot at and missed by changing Places
and being immediately at some distance and
then out of sight, as they related.'

Chamberlayn was careful to distinguish between what
he had heard and what he had seen. He says nothing
about familiars, and has no theories to account for the
phenomena. A hundred years earlier we might have
been solemnly told that the cat had been hit, and that
a track of bloody paw-marks had led straight to the
house where a suspected witch, now restored to her
human form, lay dying.

Persecution of witches and their cats continued
throughout Europe, England and America, and it was
only in 1749 that the last witch was executed, a nun
from Bavaria who was accused and found guilty of
owning three cats that were believed to be demons.

Various traditions of cruelty towards cats continued
until as far as the nineteenth century. In Ypres there

was a festival known as the 'Kattestot', which originally consisted of a great meal followed by a ceremony in which live cats were hurled from the top of the town tower to the applause and cheering of the crowds below. When a cat survived the ordeal it was said by the townsfolk that it must have been innocent and would bring a good harvest the following year.

This unkind event was discontinued in 1817, but today there is a Festival of Cats which takes place every three years. Instead of live cats, there are carnival floats with large feline effigies of all shapes and sizes. The festival also depicts a symbolic burning of witches accompanied by firework displays. It remains a curious representation of the contradictory regard for the cat in history, a celebration of its past persecution.

The late Middle Ages saw the first scholarly tomes of natural histories and bestiaries on animal anatomy begin to emerge. The cat featured prominently, analysed for its hunting abilities as much as its use as an ingredient in the treatment of diseases.

Chapter 5

TUDOR, SHAKESPEAREAN & STUART CATS OF MIXED FORTUNE

By the Middle Ages cats had become great companions for humans, but over the subsequent centuries their status varied dramatically. By the time William Shakespeare (1564-1616) was born the stalwart work of cats in helping to rid Britain of the Black Death was distant history, and he had died thirty years before the Great Plague of London. Shakespeare therefore lived at a time when cats were vilified and persecuted by the Church for their devilish associations.

It is not surprising, therefore, that there are few kindly references to cats in Shakespeare's works. He is recorded as commenting that the household cat not only lapped the milk that had been put out for it but stole the cream that hadn't. He had also written without either praise or condemnation of the cat's hunting prowess. He describes how with eyes of 'burning coal crouch before the mouse's hole', she stalked her prey.

Shakespeare has nothing to say about the cat's loving nature to man. Instead he writes with feeling about the sharpness of a cat's claws when he describes how Lysander, in *A Midsummer Night's Dream*, unkindly exclaims when trying to escape from the clinging hands of Hermia, 'Hang off, thou cat, thou burr'.

Shakespeare knew all the current cat proverbs of his time. He was familiar with the saying that a cat has nine lives, that cats can be killed by care, that a cat let 'I dare not wait upon I would' when she wanted to catch fish without wetting her paws. There was another less familiar adage, 'Good liquor will make a cat speak'. Of this Stephano must have been thinking when he offered Caliban his bottle in *The Tempest*. 'Open your mouth: here is that which will give language to you, cat.'

There are some scholars who believe Shakespeare may have actually had an antipathy to cats, a suggestion that occurs in *All's Well that Ends Well*. Bertram suffered from one. He shows it when he expresses his rising aversion to Parolles: 'I could endure anything before but a cat and now he's a cat to me'; 'more and more a cat'; 'a pox on him, he's a cat still'. Thersites in *Troilus and Cressida* lumps together 'a dog, a mule, a cat, a fitchew, a toad, a lizard, an owl, a puttock'. The fitchew was a polecat. The Queen in *Cymbeline*, discussing with Dr Cornelius her desire to experiment with deadly poisons, seeks to reassure him by a promise that she will try the forces of his compounds on such creatures as were 'counted not worth the hanging'. By this he took her to mean cats and dogs: and there is a sense of compunction in Cornelius's warning to her that she would 'from this practice but make hard her heart'.

There are only two allusions to cats in the Roman plays, both in *Coriolanus*. Marcius tells Cominius how the besieged Volscians had beaten the Romans back to their trenches and remarks angrily that

'the mouse ne'er shunned the cat as they
did budge from rascals worse than they'.

Volumnia, when heaping reproaches on Brutus after the banishment of her son, told him that it was Brutus himself who had incensed the rabble:

'Cats, that can judge as fitly of his worth
As I can of those mysteries which heaven
Will not have earth to know.'

In *Romeo and Juliet*, Mercutio, when deriding Tybalt in conversation with Benvolio, called him a 'prince of cats' when he forced a duel upon this 'lisping, affecting fantastico', this 'rat-catcher'. Tybalt then asked him, 'What wouldst thou have with me? Mercutio answers, 'Good king of cats, nothing but one of your nine lives', and when, owing to Romeo's ill-timed though well-meant intervention, Tybalt gave him – with the cat-image still in his mind – what he called 'a scratch, a scratch', almost his last thought found utterance in the bitter cry, 'Zounds, a dog, a rat, a mouse, a cat, to scratch a man to death!'

Romeo loved cats no better than Mercutio did, or the Queen in *Cymbeline*. Many mice must have haunted the rush-strewn floors of Renaissance houses, and more than a few cats must have been needed to keep them down. Hence in *Romeo and Juliet*, the banished lover's cry to Friar Lawrence:

> '– heaven is here
> Where Juliet lives; and every cat and dog
> And little mouse, every unworthy thing,
> Lives here in heaven and may look on her.'

Cats fared no better with Shakespeare's immortals. They, too, thought poorly of the cat and ranked it as an 'unworthy thing'. When Oberon, in *A Midsummer*

Night's Dream, mentions the various unlikable animals that Titania might conceivably take for his true love on waking from an enchanted slumber, he says:

> 'Be it mouse, or cat, or bear,
> Pard or boar with bristled hair.'

Elsewhere there are several allusions to cats. In *Henry IV Part One*, Falstaff proclaimed he was 'as melancholy as a Gib cat or a lugged bear'. Westmorland in *Henry V* spoke of the 'weasel Scot' playing the mouse in absence of the cat and making havoc among the princely eggs of the English eagle. This drew from Exeter the witless retort that 'it follows then the cat must stay at home'; and the zoological and metaphorical confusion was complete. Most famous of all Shakespearean cats is Hotspur's kitten in *Henry IV Part One*. In one scene the kitten was invoked to emphasise Shakespeare's dislike of 'mincing poetry'.

> 'I had rather be a kitten and cry 'mew'
> Than one of these same metre ballad-mongers.'

There are no cats in the Sonnets, but in *The Rape of Lucrece*, Tarquin is compared to 'a foul, night-walking cat'.

Unlike Shakespeare, John Skelton (1460-1529), poet and Henry VIII's tutor, was a cat lover. However, furious at the murder of his sparrow Phillip by his cat Gyb, he wrote:

'That vengaunce I aske and crye,
By way of exclamacyon,
On all the hole nacyon
Of cattes wylde and take
God send them sorowe and shame!
That cat specyally,
That slew so cruelly
My lytell prety sparowe
That I brought up at Carowe'

Cats were welcomed by many who were confined, like Henry Wriothesley, the third Earl of Southampton (1573-1624), who was incarcerated in the Tower of London at the beginning of the seventeenth century.

Lord Southampton was a friend and early patron of Shakespeare. When this foppish and futile nobleman was imprisoned in the Tower by the Queen [Elizabeth I] for his complicity in the rebellion of the Earl of Essex he commissioned a painting by John de Critz the elder. In the painting Lord Southampton looks very

Lady with a Cat, by Francesco Ubertini (1494-1557).

wan and melancholy, but fortunately he had not been totally abandoned. By his side sits Trixie, a fine black-and-white cat, the sharer of his solitude and his comforter in captivity. Trixie's journey to the Tower hadn't been easy, when Lord Southampton had first been sentenced he hadn't been able to take the cat with him. However, Trixie found him and shared his life.

Sir Henry Wyat (1460-1536), who was imprisoned in the Tower of London in the sixteenth century, also had a cat. Sir Henry wasn't as fortunate as Lord Southampton and was confined to a dungeon. The authorities were determined that Sir Henry should have it rough while in the Tower. He was not to be given much food and nor was he to have any means of keeping himself warm. The cat thwarted the authorities. He caught pigeons and brought them back for his master's supper. Sir Henry explained to his gaolers that their orders were to provide only short rations for him, but there had been no instructions that they weren't to cook. The gaolers thereafter

Opposite: A girl makes a garland watched by her pet cat. The scroll bearing the inscription 'I am here, do not forget me' is addressed to her sweetheart. Wooden panel by Hans Süss von Kulmbach, (1480-1521).

cooked the pigeons. The cat slept with Sir Henry and helped him to keep warm throughout the long nights.

Sir Philip Sidney (1554-1586), poet, literary figure and soldier who died in battle when only thirty-two was also capable of taking a cat to his heart. Sidney made an allusion to the many prejudices about cats and described an 'ugly cat' as an unlucky thing to see. Although Sidney associates cats with the idea of melancholy, in the *Arcadia*, during a dialogue between Nico and Pas, two somewhat unconvincing characters, he paints a touching picture of his own pet.

'I have (and long shall have) a white, great nimble cat,
A King upon a mouse, a strong foe to the rat.
Fine ears, long taile he hath, with Lion's curbèd clawe,
Which oft the lifteth uy and stayes his lifted pawe.
Deep musing to himselfe, which after mewing showes,
Till with lickt bearde his eye of fire espie his foes.'

Despite the traditional association with witches and spinsters, the cat seems to have been just as great a favourite with men than with women. Among the famous men who savoured her society was the great essayist and novelist Michel Eyquem de Montaigne (1533-1592). A hermit by nature, Montaigne allowed only his cat Madame Vanity to be freely admitted to a tower that he built for himself as a refuge from all human contacts. Montaigne, in 1580, succinctly describes the relationship between human and animal and writes with great modesty: 'When my cat and I entertain each other with mutual apish tricks, as playing with a garter, who knows, but I make the cat more sport than she makes me? Shall I conclude that she has her time to bein or refuse to play as freely as I have myself? Nay, who knows but that it is a defect of not understanding her language (for doubtless cats talk, and reason with one another) that we agree no better? And who knows but that she pities me for being no wiser than to play with her, and laugh and censures my folly for making sport with her, when we two play together?'

The persecution of cats was by no means universal and was not confined to any one country. Despite the ongoing persecution of cats during the period from all sections of society because of their association with witchcraft and the devil, some members of the Church were famously besotted with them. In France, Prime Minister and advisor to King Louis XIII, Cardinal Richelieu (1585-1642) appears to have held a widely contrasting attitude towards the cat. Although he was a passionate persecutor of witches and their familiars, he had at least fourteen cats of his own. Richelieu was besotted by his own pets to the extent that they were allowed to sleep in his bed, eat off his dining table and live in a room set aside for them beside his bedroom.

Richelieu's cats had individual natures. His favourite, Soumise, who often slept on Richelieu's lap, was gentle and docile, while another, named Cruel, was of a wild disposition and spent his days chasing rats. Serpolet would spend hours basking in the sun at the window, while two cats named Pyrame and Thisbe would sleep wrapped around each other. Richelieu's cats varied as much in their colours and coats as in their natures. Mimi-Papillon was a beautiful Angora, while Felimare was striped and Lucifer 'black as jet'. Sadly, after the Cardinal's death in 1642, his wishes for his beloved cats were cruelly ignored. All of them were slaughtered by the Swiss Guard, who burnt them to death just as the Cardinal himself had ordered so many witches' cats to be killed during his lifetime.

Cardinal Richelieu's counterpart in England at the

Opposite: Cardinal Richelieu and his famous collection of cats, taken from *Les Animaux Historiques*, based on the *Letters of C.G.Leroy*, by Ortaire Fournier, Paris, 1861.

time, Archbishop Laud, defied popular superstition as well as his opponents in the Church by cherishing a family of multi-coloured cats. It is said he took great delight in their company and they stalked behind the prelate as he walked in procession at Canterbury. John Aubrey remarked that the Archbishop was 'a great lover of Catts', and that he was presented with some 'Cypruss' or tabby cats, which were 'sold at first for £5 a piece'. Tabbies are still called 'Cypruss cats' in Norfolk to this day.

Although the seventeenth century was the zenith in witchcraft, and witches and the witches' cats continued to be subjected to cruelty and were vilified in their association with the devil, cats never entirely lost their popularity. They still performed an essential role around the farmyard or cottage garden where they kept the rat and mice populations in check, they went to sea and they were the companions of many people from all walks of life. The hearth-cat, whether lying upon a Turkish carpet in the withdrawing-room or upon the warm flagstones before the kitchen fire, was a creature loved by many.

Public contempt of the cat co-existed with distaste and even ridicule in some quarters. Francois Augustin Paradis de Moncrif (1687-1770), poet and dramatist, is well known as the first writer to document the cat in detail. His greatest work on the subject of cats, *Les Chats*, now revered as the first of all great cat books, was originally published in 1727. It is a passionate defence of the animal in respect of its greatest critics. Despite his honourable intentions Moncrif was jeered and mocked when his writings first appeared and cruel satires were launched in response. Eventually, as a result of public pressure as well as ridicule from his academic peer group, Moncrif was forced to withdraw *Les Chats* from sale altogether.

There were other, equally unkind stories. In the

Illustration of a cat's tomb taken from Moncrif's *Les Chats*, 1727. Just as today, in the seventeenth and eighteenth centuries it was popular for an adored pet to be buried in a pet cemetery and a memorial erected in his or her memory.

year of Shakespeare's death, Thomas Tomkins (1572-
1656) of Trinity College, Cambridge, wrote a play
entitled *Patho-Machia or the Battell of the Affections* where he
introduces the audience to certain 'factious men',

> 'where of one of late killed his cat because it
> killed a Mouse on Sunday.'

This tale circulated well into the seventeenth century.

Thomas Master, friend and literary assistant of
Lord Herbert of Cherbury, inserts the same story into
his poem, *Lute-Strings Cat-Eaten*. In the depth of the
night the cat gnawed the strings of Master's ivory-
inlaid lute until only a few pathetic shreds of them
remained. His poem describes his reaction at finding
the cat had destroyed the lute.

> 'He will curse her for it.
> May she dwell with some dry hermit,
> where rat ne'er peeped, where mouse ne'er fed',
> or with some 'close-pared brother'
> with whom she must either fast on Sunday
> or else be hanged the day after.'

In truth, Master was devoted to the cat and whatever her

motivation at destroying the lute strings she was forgiven, just as he forgave her all her mischievous behaviour.

The continuing association of the cat with magic and witchcraft led to its increasing use in alchemy and medicine. A tail of a black cat rubbed onto the eye was often thought to cure a sty. Edward Topsell's *History of Four-footed Beasts and Serpents,* a serious academic work on natural history written in 1607 and reprinted in 1658 mentions a number of cures using different parts of a cat's anatomy. He recommends in the treatment of gout taking the fat of a cat and anointing the sick part with it; for blindness Topsell suggests taking the head of a black cat, burnt to a fine dust. With a quill the

The Domestic Cat, *A General History of Quadrupeds,* published in 1807 in Newcastle-upon-Tyne, by Thomas Berwick (1753-1828). In the work four types of cats are described.

powder should be blown into the eye three times a day. For convulsions 'a powder made of the gall of a black cat' is thought to be the most effective cure. For inducing a still birth Topsell suggests taking 'the gall of a cat with the black dung of the same cat' and burning it in perfume beneath a woman carrying a dead child.

A sinister and dismissive role may have been attributed to some cats, but others were the objects of devotion. King Charles I, King of Scotland from 1625 to 1649 is said to have owned a lucky black cat that died before the King's arrest that led to his trial and execution in the Civil War.

Samuel Pepys (1633-1703), the famous diarist, had held a number of internationally important positions. He was cynical, practical and realistic, but

The 17th century image of the Wild Cat from the *Historaie Naturalis* by Johannes Johnstanus, 1657.

once allowed himself to imagine, but only for a few moments and in unusual circumstances, that his 'young Gib cat' might be a ghost and have supernatural powers. At 7 a.m. on the morning of November 29, 1667, Mr and Mrs Pepys were roused from sleep by some frighteningly peculiar noises – knockings, sounds as of furniture being moved about and the sound of footsteps, as it seemed to Mr and Mrs Pepys tucked up in bed, as if someone was going up and down the stairs.

Summoning up his courage Mr Pepys at last left the security of his bed, pulled on his breeches, wrapped a gown about him and took a firebrand in his hand, He opened the bedroom-door. The noise had now stopped, and there was nothing to be seen. He then woke Jane, his maid. She said that she had also been 'afeared'; but, being more stout-hearted than their master, she and a fellow-servant had investigated it. They found nothing stirring except the cook, already at her post in the kitchen. Jane the maid pointed out that the noise had come from the recently swept chimney stack of their neighbour, Sir John Minnes' house. Pepys was never certain about what had occurred and always declared that it was one of the most extraordinary incidents in his life. On the occasion when his Gib-cat leapt from the top to the bottom of his stairs in a couple of bounds, his memories of the unexplained sounds came back to him and for a moment he feared that what he was hearing was a ghost, and that his house was truly haunted.

Cats also played a prominent part in the many fables written during this period, when they were often seen as clever, mischievous and wise. John Gay's (1685-1732) twenty-first fable tells of a house grievously plundered by rats and of a housemaid, Betty, who 'cursed the Cat for want of duty'. A professional rat-catcher was engaged, a 'man of wondrous skill', who planned his campaigning with care, sought out the habits and the haunts of the pests, and proceeded to lay his well-baited traps in all the likeliest places. The dispossessed cat followed him round, perceiving that if he should flourish 'The purring race must be undone'.

The cat, believing it thought it knew a trick, secretly removed the bait from every trap. Finding himself thus frustrated, the vermin exterminator proceeded to take counter-measures. He brought a ponderous trap of unusual size, baited it with judgment – and succeeded in catching the cat. In vain the cat mewed piteously for pardon; in vain it pleaded that he should spare 'a sister of the science'. The vermin exterminator retorted, unmoved, that if the whole of the cat's 'interloping band' were banished his calling would raise its fees and, indeed, establish a monopoly.

At this point an older and wiser cat intervened with a powerful argument. 'Two of a trade', she observed, 'have never agreed'. 'Squires, beauties, kings, all envy and assail each other. Why should not cats and rat-catchers show greater wisdom, limit their desires, and accept the fact that there is 'game' enough for them all?' The fable ends there: but one may hope that the rat-catcher was convinced, and that the 'pondrous trap' opened its jaws at last.

The familiar figure of the cat-loving crone reappears in Gay's twenty-third fable, sitting in 'a little smoky flame', mumbling her prayers backwards and surrounded by lank and mewing cats. Annoyed by their din, the 'untamed scold of fourscore years' most unfairly rounds on them. If they had not been 'housed and nursed', she would never have been pursued by yelling boys, crossed straws would not have been laid athwart her path, horseshoes would not have been nailed to the doors of houses to protect the inhabitants from her spells, nor would the wenches have hidden away their brooms 'for fear that she might up and ride'. One of the cats has a retort ready. If they had not lived meagrely beneath her roof they could have lived 'with credit' as 'beasts of chase'.

> 'Tis infamy to serve a hag;
> Cats are thought imps, her broom a nag;
> And boys against our lives combine
> Because 'tis thought *your* cats have nine.'

La Fontaine, (1621-95), whether borrowing from the early fable authors or using his own inventive powers, is often more sophisticated in his approach. Fontaine is keenly conscious of the value of a cat as an actor, such as in *The Cock, the Cat and the Little Mouse*.

The mouse, a very young and ingenuous mouselet, came running to its mother to describe two strange creatures whom he had just encountered. One was graceful and benignant-looking; the other, active and alarming. This second beast had a shrill, fierce voice, two arm-like things with which he beat the air, a tail like a flaunting knightly plume, and a piece of flesh on the top of his head. The little mouse would have fled from this outlandish being had he not felt reassured by the presence of the more amiable stranger, whose fur was as soft as his own, who was prettily striped, had a long tail, and bore on its face a mild, modest expression, though its eyes certainly did glow. Moreover, it seemed well disposed towards mice, and the bold infant would have spoken to it had not a sudden blare of noise from 'the other' sent him scurrying away. 'My son,' then said the Mother Mouse, 'that gentle creature was a *cat*. Under its hypocritical airs it nourishes an inextinguishable feud against all our family. Your "other", on the contrary, far from doing us any harm, may some day provide us with a dinner, for he is a *cock*. As for your cat, it is *we* who would do the providing.'

'*Moral*:

As long as you may live beware
Of judging people by their air.'

The Cat and Cock, illustration by Francis Barlow (1626-1702) taken from *Aesop's Fables with His Life*, London, 1666. The cat resembles a fox pouncing on his prey in this rural scene.

Another slightly later writer of fables, Edward Moore, (1712-57) in the ninth of those he dedicated to Caroline of Anspach, Princess of Wales, describes a 'jolly farmer' seated at table and sharing titbits with his favourite spaniel. When in her turn the cat seeks a share, the dog protests that

> 'They only earn a right to eat
> Who earn by services their meat.'

He waxes eloquent on the theme of his own exertions, springing and retrieving the game, defending his master's flock from wolves and his house from robbers.

The idea of the cat as a symbol of man's cunning and intelligence was developed in the well-known seventeenth-century folktale of *Puss in Boots*, written down by lawyer and writer Charles Perrault (1628-1703). Along with other traditional folk tales such as *Cinderella*, *Sleeping Beauty* and *Little Red Riding Hood*, *Puss in Boots* presented a very different image of the cat as witch's familiar and representation of evil.

Opposite: Girl with a Kitten, by French artist Jean-Baptiste Perronneau (1715-1783). While some cats continued to be villified, others were enjoying a renaissance as family pets.

Kitten by George Stubbs (1724-1806). Stubbs is renowned for his paintings of horses. He also made numerous studies of dogs, but this portrait of a kitten, which belonged to a young girl named Anne White is the only known picture of a cat by him.

The tale is of a young man whose only possession is his cat and who, out of desperation since he has no money, plans to eat the cat and wear its skin. The cat cleverly manages to persuade his owner that all will be well if he only has a pair of boots made for him and a small pouch to carry. Puss then catches a rabbit and presents it as a gift to the King on behalf of his master and in gratitude the King introduces the master to the daughter. The couple live happily ever after and Puss retires from his mousing, achieving great fame and eminence. Such a tale of good fortune because of the cat's actions had a profoundly positive influence on the reputation of the cat throughout Europe and it was later taken up by music hall entertainers as a well-known pantomime in the nineteenth century.

Cats didn't only appear in legends and literature. Sir Isaac Newton, the great mathematician and physicist, (1642-1727), also had many other interests. He had been a Member of Parliament for Cambridge University and Master of the Mint. Aside from his public life he was fascinated by the study of religion and was a cat lover. The story that is best remembered is that when he had two cats, one rather plump and large and the other rather thin and athletic, he insisted on having two cat flaps cut into his door. He didn't

Puss in Boots, by Gustave Doré (1832-1883). Doré's engraving illustrated an 1862 edition of Perrault's fairy tales, *Histoires ou contes du temps passe*, a collection of eight classic and traditional tales that included *Sleeping Beauty*, *Bluebeard* and *Puss in Boots*.

want either cat to think that they were less important than the other.

Elsewhere during the period, cats continued a long tradition featuring in art. Mary, Queen of Scots, busied herself with the tapestry hangings which she and her then custodian, Bess of Shrewsbury, were embroidering together. Mary Queen of Scots traced with her needle the likeness of a grim Graymalkin cat, bushy-whiskered and glaring-eyed. This 'catte' (as Mary has carefully labelled her) sits primly, gazing straight ahead. The kink at the top of her tail suggests that it is beginning to twitch in a manner that bodes ill to the fat rodent (more like a rat than a mouse) as it steals away.

Two Girls Dressing a Kitten by Candlelight, by Joseph Wright of Derby (1734–1797).

Chapter 6

GEORGIAN LITERARY CATS OF ELEGANCE & DEVOTION

The eighteenth century was an age not only of great literature, but of great literary cat lovers, including Horace Walpole, Thomas Gray, Christopher Smart and William Cowper.

Samuel Johnson (1709-1784) is remembered not only as a man of letters and as a lexicographer, but as a cat lover. He lavished attention on the cat. He was not the sort of man to be content to buy cat's meat from the itinerant trader, for Dr Johnson went himself to the fish market to buy oysters for Hodge, his treasured companion. Oysters at the time were not the luxury food they are today, but were considered to be especially nutritious. The reason he chose to buy Hodge's food himself was that he feared that had he left it to his servants, they would have been disgruntled by the extra work required of them. He wanted no one to have a poor opinion of Hodge.

Perhaps Johnson had learnt from Boswell's approach to cats that not everybody could share his love and admiration for his feline friend.

James Boswell (1740-1795) admitted that when he was with Johnson and Hodge, he always felt a shade nervous about the cat's presence. Boswell wrote in his own diary, 'I'm uneasy with a cat in the room and I frequently suffered a good deal from the presence of the same Hodge.' In his biography of Johnson, Boswell describes how when he admired Hodge one day, he was forward enough to suggest that as cats go Hodge was a really fine specimen. Johnson replied that Hodge was indeed a fine cat, but that he had owned finer ones. Johnson, feeling that he had let Hodge down with his faint praise, then proceeded to extol the cat's virtues.

William Cowper (1731-1800) was a poet who throughout his life experienced difficulties with his relationships with other people. Bereft by the death of his mother in early childhood, later disappointed in love, before again being left alone after the death of his close friend and companion Mary Unwin, he became increasingly depressed. He wrote of man's helplessness and isolation and was forever seeking a life of domestic bliss and rural solitude, which he never succeeded in finding. He sought solace in the company of animals. He enjoyed the company of his spaniel, three pet hares, his cats and their kittens.

Cowper never regarded cats in quite the same light as dogs and it is striking that whereas his dogs had names, his cats remained nameless. However, the cats in his poetry were named. Hodge, Selima and Jeffry have become characters in Britain's literary heritage. Accounts of their life give an insight into life in Olney, Bedfordshire, where he lived and the important role that cats played in a household. Cowper's cats were able to come and go at will through an early cat flap, and there is plenty of evidence that his cats lived a pampered life. Even so, Cowper has been criticized for not being at heart a dedicated cat lover. It is said that each of his poems reveals a flaw in the poet's 'catmanity', as opposed to humanity.

The incident that inspired the writing of the poem *The Colubriad* was related by Cowper in a letter to the Rev. William Unwin, dated August 3rd, 1782. William Unwin was the former husband of Mrs Unwin who had been so kind to Cowper up to her death.

'Passing from the greenhouse into the barn I saw three kittens (we have so many in our retinue) looking with fixed attention at something which lay on the threshold of a door coiled up. I took but little notice of them at first but a loud hiss engaged me to attend more closely, when behold, a viper! The largest I remember to have seen, rearing itself, darting its forked tongue and ejaculating the aforementioned hiss at the nose of a kitten almost in contact with his lips. I ran into the hall for a hoe with a long handle, with which I intended to assail him, and returning in a few seconds missed him: he was gone and I feared had escaped me. Still however the kitten sat watching immovably on the same spot. I concluded therefore that, sliding between the door and the threshold, he had found his way out of the garden into the yard. I went round immediately and there found him in close conversation with the old cat, whose curiosity being excited by so novel an appearance, inclined her to pat his head repeatedly with her fore-foot; with her claws however sheathed, and not in anger, but in the way of philosophical enquiry and examination.

To prevent her falling a victim to so laudable an exercise of her talents, I interposed

Portrait of Ambroise Louis Garneray by Jean Francois
Garneray (1783–1857).

in a moment with the hoe and performed upon him an act of decapitation which, though not immediately mortal, proved so in the end. Had he slid into the passages, where it is dark, or had he, when in the yard, met no interruption from the cat and secreted himself in one of the outhouses, it is hardly possibly but that some of the family must have been bitten.'

His first anxiety, before he had time to imagine the viper's stealthy escape into the dark passages or its invasion of the outhouses beyond, was lest the sinister creature should deprive the household of their only cat 'that was of age to combat with a rat'. He dealt energetically with the crisis:

'With outstretched hoe I slew him at the door
And taught him NEVER TO COME
THERE NO MORE.'

Six years later, when he had moved from Olney, with its bleak marketplace and the overgrown garden at Orchard Side, he wrote to his cousin, Lady Hesketh, from Western Lodge, his final Buckinghamshire home.

The letter reveals that he wasn't entirely unresponsive to a kitten's charms, even if it also implied that he lacked enthusiasm for some grown cats.

> 'I have a kitten, my dear, the drollest of all creatures that ever wore a cat's skin. Her gambols are not to be described and would be incredible if they could. In point of size she is likely to be a kitten always, being extremely small of her age, but time, I suppose, that spoils everything, will make her a cat. You will see her, I hope, before that melancholy period shall arrive, for no wisdom that she may gain by experience and reflection hereafter will compensate the loss of her present hilarity.
>
> She is dressed in a tortoise-shell suit and I know that you will delight in her.'

Horace Walpole (1717-97) was known as being a dog-lover from childhood and later became famous for his affinity to cats. His fondness for cats may well have grown more gradually than his attachment to dogs. Certainly he displayed a sorry lack of enthusiasm for Maltese cats in his early twenties. After Walpole returned to London from the grand tour in Italy, he was at a dinner party when a guest excitedly mentioned the fine Maltese cats. The cats had been bred by a Prussian exile named Stosch. Walpole wrote at once to Sir Horace Mann about his friend Lord Islay's interest in Maltese cats: 'Lord Islay begged I would write to Florence to have the largest male and female that could be got. If you will speak to Stosch you will oblige me. They may come by sea.' In May of the ensuing year he wrote again: 'I laughed very much at the family of cats I am to receive. I believe they will be extremely welcome to Lord Islay, for he appears little, lives more darkly and more like a wizard than ever. These huge cats will figure prodigiously in his cell.'

Two months later they were 'those odious cats of Malta', not because of any intrinsic fault in the cats but because their transportation was proving so difficult. Fortunately, Walpole's soft spot for all animals overcame the problem. 'Oh, the cats! I can never keep them, and yet it is barbarous to send them all to Lord Islay. He will shut them up and starve them, and then bury them under the stairs with his wife.' The Maltese cats that had raised both the hopes and then the ire of those who had hoped to receive them never materialised. But by then Walpole had

An eighteenth-century painting in inks from an album in the style of the Korean artist Chong Sung (1676-1759).

other cats and he had become the Earl of Orford. In 1743 Walpole moved to his father's house in Arlington Street and this remained his house for the next thirty-seven years. He had brought his cats from Norfolk.

Walpole could not settle anywhere without his dogs and his cats. His two cats, Zara and Selima, formed part of his household and soon became as familiar to his friends as his books and china.

In February, 1747, a sad fate overtook one of the cats; she was, as later generations well know, 'drowned in a tub of goldfishes'. On learning of this disaster his friend the poet Thomas Gray (1716-1771) wrote a letter of condolence from Cambridge:

> 'As one ought to be particularly careful to avoid blunders in a compliment of condolence, it would be a sensible satisfaction to me (before I testify my sorrow and the sincere part I take in your misfortune) to know for certain who it is I lament. I knew Zara and Selima, (Selima, was it, or Fatima?) or rather I knew them both together; for I cannot justly say which was which. Then as to your handsome Cat, the name you distinguish her by, I am no less at a loss, as well knowing

one's handsome cat is always the cat one likes best; or, if one be alive and the other dead, it is usually the latter that is the handsomest. Oh, no! I would rather seem to mistake, and imagine to be sure it must be the tabby one that had met with this sad accident. Till this affair is a little better determined you will excuse me if I do not begin to cry.'

He may not have begun to cry; but before he closed the letter he added the *Ode* on *feue Mademoiselle Selime* which would immortalize her not 'for one week or fortnight' as he modestly foretold, but for all time.

'Twas on a lofty vase's side
Where China's gayest art had dyed
The azure flowers that blow;
Demurest of the tabby kind,
The pensive Selima reclined,
Gazed on the lake below.

Her conscious tail her joy declared,
The fair round face, the snowy beard,
The velvet of her paws,
Her coat, that with the tortoise vies,

Her ears of jet and emerald eyes,
She saw; and purred applause.

Still had she gazed; but 'midst the tide
Two angel forms were seen to glide,
The genii of the stream;
Their scaly armour's Tyrian hue
Through richest purple to the view
Betrayed a golden gleam.

The hapless nymph with wonder saw;
A whisker first and then a claw
With many an ardent wish
She stretched, in vain, to reach the prize.
What female heart can gold despise,
What cat's averse to fish?

Presumptuous Maid! with looks intent,
Again she stretched, again she bent,
Nor knew the gulf between.
(Malignant Fate sat by and smiled)
The slippery verge her feet beguiled,
She tumbled headlong in.
Eight times emerging from the flood,
She mewed to every watery god

Some speedy aid to send.
No Dolphin came, no Nereid stirred,
No cruel Tom or Susan heard,
A Favourite has no friend.

From hence, ye Beauties, undeceived,
Know one false step is ne'er retrieved,
And be with caution bold.
Not all that tempts your wandering eyes
And heedless hearts is lawful prize,
Nor all that glitters gold.'

Walpole was immensely proud that a cat of his should have been honoured in a poem by someone he admired as much as Gray. After Grays' death he enthroned the 'lofty vase', the funeral urn of Selima, on a pedestal at Strawberry Hill, engraved with the first six lines of the *Ode*, only altering the first to 'Twas on *this* lofty vase's side.

Christopher Smart (1722-1771) is the final member of this group of literary cat lovers, and is better remembered as a friend of Dr Johnson than for his quality as a poet. Smart's reputation as a poet relies on one poem only, his *Song of David*. A fellow of Pembroke College, Cambridge, Smart's finances fell into ruin and he eventually fell ill and was admitted to an asylum in

The Cat of Kazan. From Russian folk art, the woodcut cartoon, known as a *lubok*, satirized Tsar Peter I the Great of Russia's many titles and his moustache. Artist unknown.

London, during which time he was befriended by a cat whom he named Jeoffry, his only companion during his time there. According to Smart, Jeoffry was worthy of being presented before the throne of grace. 'I will', he announces, 'consider my cat Jeoffry. For he is the servant of the living God and daily serving Him'. These lines were set to music much later in the twentieth century by Sir Benjamin Britten.

Smart describes in detail how Jeoffry, on waking in the morning 'wreathes his body seven times round with elegant quickness', sharpens his claws, washes himself, looks up for instructions, goes off in quest of food. Jeoffry, he writes, 'keeps the Lord's watch in the night against the adversary – he counteracts the powers of darkness by his electrical skin and glaring eyes – in the morning orisons [prayers] he loves the sun and the sun loves him'.

It was by stroking Jeoffry that Christopher Smart 'found out electricity'. He tells us that Jeoffry 'has the subtlety and hissing of the serpent, which in goodness he suppresses. For he will not do destruction if he is well fed, neither will he spit without provocation. For he purrs with thankfulness when God tells him he is a good cat. For he is an instrument for the children to learn benevolence upon. For every house is incomplete without him and blessing is lacking in the spirit.'

'The English cats are the best in Europe,' declares Smart, but it is upon one particular English cat that his wandering mind is focused. 'He is a mixture of gravity and waggery ... there is nothing sweeter than his peace when he is at rest. There is nothing brisker than his life when he is in motion.' His tongue is exceeding pure, so that it possesses in purity what it lacks in music. Moreover, God had blest him with a variety of movements, so that, though he could not fly, he was an excellent clamberer.'

Smart finally died penniless in a debtor's prison in 1771 and it is not known what happened to Jeoffry.

It was in the eighteenth century that the term 'tom cat' was originally coined to refer to a male domestic cat. Before then a male cat was referred to as a 'ram' or a 'boar'. An anonymously written work of fiction entitled *The Life and Adventures of a Cat* was published in 1760 containing a hero named 'Tom' and became so successful that the term 'tom' came into general usage and has been commonplace for the last two hundred and fifty years.

Another saying absorbed into the English language during this period was the everyday expression 'it is raining cats and dogs'. This euphemistic saying originated when little or no drainage existed in streets and alleyways in city areas. When a downpour arrived there was frequently nowhere for the water to to flow. Heavy storms often produced substantial flooding and it was not uncommon for the cats and dogs on the roadside to be swept away and drowned, often in great quantity. Jonathan Swift, writing in 1710, observed the 'swelling kennels' washing up their 'trophies' - 'drowned puppies, stinking sprats, all drenched in mud, dead cats, and turnip tops'.

Self-Portrait with the Bust of Homer, by John Kay (1742-1826). Kay said of the print that he described himself in a thoughtful posture; his favourite cat, believed to be the largest in Scotland, sitting on the back of his chair.

Illustration of *Puss in Boots* by Gustave Doré (1832-1883).

Chapter 7

SOME LITERARY & ARTISTIC CATS OF THE ROMANTIC AGE

Many of the well-known Romantic poets took great comfort and solace from their feline companions. Lord Byron (1788-1824) owned five cats, among other animals, and was known to feed the stray cats while on his travels in Ravenna in Italy. Charlotte Brontë (1816-1855) and Emily Brontë (1818-1848) both completely adored their pet cats. Emily's cat Tiger would play at her feet while she wrote *Wuthering Heights*.

In 1844 when Charlotte wrote to her friend Ellen Nussey she was careful to present an image of Emily playing with her cat. Both girls were well aware that Emily held animals dearly and were considered almost as important to her as humans. She also wrote on the occasion the cat died: 'Monday morning. Our poor little cat has been ill for two days, and is just dead. It is piteous to see an animal laying lifeless'. On another occasion Emily described her thoughts about cats within an essay entitled *Le Chat*, addressed to M. Heger. It was dated May 15 1842.

'I can say with sincerity that I like cats; I can also give very good reasons why those who hate them are wrong. A cat is an animal which has more human feelings than almost any other being. We cannot stand up under comparison with the dog, he is infinitely too good; but the cat, although he differs in some physical traits, is extremely like us in disposition.

'In truth there may be people who would say that the resemblance is close only to the meanest human beings, that it is limited to their excessive hypocrisy, cruelty and ingratitude – detestable vices in our race and equally odious in the cat's. Without disputing the limits which these individuals place on our affinity, I answer, if that hypocrisy, cruelty and ingratitude are the characteristics exclusively of mean people, this class includes everyone; our education develops one of these qualities to great perfection, the others thrive without cultivation, and we, far from condemning them, look upon all three with great complaisance.

'A cat, for his own interest, sometimes hides his misanthropy under appearance of most endearing gentleness; instead of scratching what he desires from his master's hand, he approaches in a caressing manner, rubs his pretty little head against him and sticks out his paw to touch as soft as down.

'This act finished, he resumes the character of Timon. Such finesse in him we call hypocrisy; but in ourselves we give it another name, politeness, and any person not using it to disguise his true feelings would soon be driven from society.

'"But," says some delicate lady who has murdered a half dozen lap dogs by sheer affection, "the cat is such a cruel beast he is not content to kill his prey, but torments it before death; you cannot bring this accusation against us."

'Pretty near, Madame. Your husband, for example, likes hunting very much, but foxes are scarce on his land; he would not be able to enjoy the sport often if he did not manage his recourses after this fashion. When he has run an animal to its last breath, he pulls it from the mouths of the dogs, and saves it to suffer the same ordeal two or three times more, ending finally in death. You yourself avoid a bloody spectacle, because it wounds your weak nerves, but I have seen you embrace your child rapturously when he came to show you a beautiful butterfly crushed between his cruel little fingers; and, at that moment, I wished very much I had a cat, with the half swallowed tail of a rat hanging from his mouth, to present as the image, the true copy of your angel. You could not refuse to kiss him also, and if he scratched us both in return, so much the better.

'Little boys are liable enough to acknowledge thus their friends' caresses, and the resemblance would be even more perfect. Cats' ingratitude is another name for shrewdness. They are able to judge our favours at their true value because they discern the motives which prompt us to bestow them; and even if these motives are sometimes good, no doubt they still remember that they owe all their wretchedness and bad qualities to the great ancestor of the human race, for surely cats in Paradise are not mean.'

In the Brontë household, as in all households where cats are treasured members of the family, the pleasure of their companionship of a cat is from time to time rudely destroyed by its death. Tiger died while Emily was in Brussels in 1845, but his companions Keeper and Flossie were fortunately alive and well. Branwell Brontë has left to posterity a drawing of a cat that is now in the Museum dedicated to the Brontë family in Haworth, Yorkshire. This may well have been one of the family cats.

Girl Holding a Cat, by Phillipe Mercier (1689–1760).

Another poet who loved cats and gained solace from their companionship while suffering from tuberculosis was Keats. Letters from John Keats (1795-1821) to his family, together with descriptions of Keats' family life make it clear that cats played a prominent part in their lives. Keats' mother is said to have had a light-coloured tabby cat. Keats' actions were as idealistic as his writing. There is a well-known story, recorded by Keats' friend Charles Cowden Clarke (1787-1877), of an occasion in Hampstead when a local butcher's boy began to torment a kitten. The butcher's boy, a brute, according to Keats, wouldn't desist, when he was challenged about his behaviour. Keats wasn't to be defeated and although at this time he must already have been suffering from tuberculosis, he set to with the brute and fought him with bare fists.

The fight continued for nearly an hour, but luckily, early on in the fray the poet had landed a blow that had made the brute reel. After this, like a skilled boxer, he concentrated on the damage he had inflicted. Keats was the victor and left his adversary so defeated that he had to be helped home. The house where this battle took place still stands and is now known as 'Keats' House'.

Two years before this epic encounter, Keats had written a sonnet in honour of another family's cat.

This cat belonged to the Reynolds family who were then living in Lamb's Conduit Street in Bloomsbury, London. This cat was elderly and wheezed. It had lost part of its tail but in his day had been a force to be reckoned with in the cat world of Bloomsbury and was a terror to the local rats and mice. Keats' description of him in the *Comic Annual* has immortalised this ageing tom.

> 'Cat! who hast passed thy grand climacteric,
> How many mice and rats hast in thy days
> Destroyed? How many titbits stolen? Gaze
> With those bright, languid segments green,
>   and prick
> Those velvet ears, but prith'ee do not stick
> Thy latent talons in me – but upraise
> Thy gentle mew and tell me all thy frays
> Of fish and mice and rats and tender chick.'

Elsewhere Keats has described how this cat was not a creature to be trifled with. He famously writes of the cat's claws as the 'latent talons'. They had apparently been used with effect against Keats on at least one occasion when they had been sunk into Keats' hand and knee. Keats was a merciful man and bore no grudge. He saw the beauty of the old hero's green eyes and velvet ears, and despite his injuries, found time to play with him and stroke him. He was surprised to find that despite the cat's age, his injuries and his wheezing chest, the fur was still as soft as it had been when a kitten.

Cats played an important role in many of the families that were visited by Keats during the last years of his life. One cat, Tom, was especially dear to him, and he loved him with all the passion of which his passionate nature was capable. Keats felt the loss of Tom deeply. In another letter to John Reynolds (1796-1852), while lying in his sick bed in Rome, Keats described the images that came before his eyes. Among these were such strange visions as Voltaire in medieval armour and Alexander the Great wearing a nightcap. There was also an hallucination of

'Old Socrates a-tying his cravat. And Hazlitt playing with Miss Edgeworth's cat.'

Percy Bysshe Shelley (1792-1822), poet, friend and supporter of Keats was also a great cat lover and prepared to battle on their behalf. Mary Shelley (1797-1851) records how in 1818 she called to her

Caricature of Olympia published in *Le Charivari*, by Edouard Manet, 1863.

husband and said 'Come and look: here's a cat eating roses; she'll turn into a woman. When beasts eat these roses they turn into men and women.'

Sir Walter Scott (1771-1832) was a lawyer by profession, but within a few years of qualifying he had published his first literary work and within ten years had become famous. He was the most popular author of his day. However busy he was, and he laboured night and day to satisfy his publishers and bankers, he still found time to enjoy his house, his family and his animals. Scott is famed for his love of dogs, it is not well known that he was also a great cat lover and he even found time for the household's pigs, hens and donkeys. Hinse of Hinsfeldt was the cat who was his constant companion when Scott was at his town house in North Castle Street, Edinburgh. The cat had owed its rather exotic name to the hero of a German fairy tale who had caught Scott's attention.

A contemporary account of Scott's library in Edinburgh has described how it was shared by Maida, one of Scott's dogs, and Hinse, his cat. The dog would lie on the hearth-rug waiting for a snap of his master's fingers when he would come and place his head upon his knee. Hinse would watch carefully and jealously from his perch at the top of the library steps. Hinse was remembered by contemporary writers who were friends of Scott's as 'venerable, fat and sleek, and no longer very locomotive'. In his younger days it is said that Hinse had been well able to hold his own against the many dogs in the household. But, by the time this description of Scott's Edinburgh library was written, Hinse preferred the dignified security of the top of the library steps. He stayed there until Maida had thumped on the library door with his huge paw as a signal that he wanted to be let out. Once the dog was out of the way Hinse was free to wander around the library and to settle on the footstool by his master's feet.

Scott was as enthusiastic about other people's cats as he was about his own. In the last year of his life when Scott was already ill from high blood pressure and circulatory problems, he travelled to Italy. Among those he visited was the Bishop of Tarentum. Scott liked him as he had, unlike many older men, remained flexible in mind and with a kind heart. Scott noted in his journal that the Bishop, even in old age, had retained an engaging youthfulness of mind and a fondness for cats that he shared with his visitor. One of the Bishop's cats was a superb Persian.

Scott wasn't the only person of note to have admired this particular cat. Lord Yarmouth (1777-1842),

Francis Charles Seymour-Ingram, another of the Bishop's visitors, has commented that although the Persian cat possessed great beauty and character, there was none quite as fine as that of the Bishop.

Lord Yarmouth and Sir Walter Scott were not the only people who have left accounts of the Bishop and his cats. Samuel Rogers (1763-1855), banker, poet, art collector and author *of The Pleasures of Memory* has used the Bishop as a character in his books and has left a portrait of an 'old cardinal' dining with his cats who appeared to be the wisest and gravest of those around the table.

Although Robert Southey (1774-1843) was a prolific writer, he is often considered one of the less important members of the group that became known as the Lakeland poets. He was a school friend of Coleridge and later became his brother-in-law. He may not have been the greatest poet, and may have been eclipsed by Wordsworth, DeQuincey and Coleridge, but he was the greatest cat lover of them all.

Southey wrote the lines that have been quoted for two hundred years by cat lovers:

'A kitten was in the animal world what a rosebud is in a garden'.

He owned a succession of cats, ending with one named Hurlyburlybuss – surely a name dreamt up by of one of the Southey children. Another of Southey's cats was named 'The Most Noble the Archduke Rumpelstilzchen, Marquis Macbum, Earle Tomemange, Baron Taricide, Waowler and Skaratchi'. Known simply as Rumpel about the Southey household, he was much mourned by the family and servants when he died.

It is not only writers who have always been cat lovers. Artists have also been devoted to them. William Hogarth (1697-1764) famously painted four charming children of Admiral Lord George Graham. In the foreground a small girl dances to the music of a bird organ, the handle of which her brother is turning. Another child holds the plump fist of the youngest of the three who sits in a low-wheeled chair and is obviously enchanted with the thrilling notes of the organ. There is a bird in the background fluttering in its cage. A large tabby cat is peering at it over the back of a chair, teeth bared and green eyes glowing.

Joseph Nollekens (1737-1823) was a sculptor who became the friend of King George III and many of the leading politicians of the time, including Fox and Pitt. He also moved in artistic and intellectual circles and was an associate of actors and writers such as Garrick, Stern,

Goldsmith and Johnson. Nollekens, who was notoriously careful with money, lived in unfashionable Mortimer Street, London, in a meagre house. There he kept a cat. It was unkindly said that rations were so short in Nollekens' house that the cat must have been an expert mouser as otherwise it would surely have died of starvation. As much as he welcomed his cat, there are no accounts of him laying out, however grudgingly, money to the cat's-meat man, much less to the fishmonger or milk man. However, unlike Cowper, he did name his cat. Nollekens' cat was known as Jenny Dawdle. Nollekens' pupils were always delighted to watch Jenny Dawdle playing among the unfinished sculptures in his studio and with 'Black Bet', Nollekens' mistress.

French artists of the late Romantic period, particularly the Impressionists, were captivated by the cat, expressing their love for the animal in great masterpieces of art. In 1895 an eminent art historian, appropriately named Professor Harvey Fishbone, was commissioned to bring together a unique collection of cat paintings from the Romantic period to be housed at the Fishbone Museum. A curator was appointed with the name of Professor Hippolyte Feline. Paul Cezanne painted *Woman with a Coffee Pot*. From Edward Degas there was *The Orchestra of the Palais Opera*, with an

Sleeping Cat, Japanese watercolour, c. 1850, artist unknown. Although the eyes are firmly shut, the ears belonging to this cat suggest the cat remains alert.

orchestra consisting entirely of cats. Paul Gauguin's *Tahitian Women* depicted exotic natives represented by cats. Manet and Monet painted dozens of cats. Manet painted Nana, a cat accompanied by a cat gentleman complete with coat tails and a cane.

In 1866 Monet gave the world *Woman in a Green Dress, Woman in a Garden, Wild Poppies* and *The Cradle* among many other masterpieces. Professor Hippolite Feline wrote: 'we may think of Monet accompanied by his own cats on a stroll in the country, realizing how the pets wander among the wild poppies with more pleasure and style than the people he has just painted'.

An equally romantic city dwelling place for the cat has always been the great city of Venice where for hundreds of years feral strays have been integral to the churchyards, parks, bridges, piers and alley ways. It is said that two merchants, Rustico de Torcello and Buono Tribuno de Malamacco first brought in the cats to Venice, to protect the merchandise on the great cargo ships entering the bay. Once in the Venetian

Opposite: The roles of mouser and rat are reversed as in this Japanese watercolour a musk-rat raja sits on a throne, holding a hookah, a pennant, above. Below him another musk-rat rides on a tame cat. c.1880.

lagoon, the cats became the guardians of the precious stocks of grain and clothes stashed in the city storehouses. Favourite cat haunts have included 'La Scala del Bobolo', 'The Stairway of the Snail', and the fish market at the Campo Santa Margherita.

Invisible during the day, the cats have always tended to come out at night, disappearing at dawn. At night for centuries they have slept in the porches and stairways of the basilicas and palazos. Cats have also been known to ride on the Santa Sophia gondolas that go to the fish market of the Rialto, returning after a meal for a happy afternoon snooze.

Just as in ancient Egypt there were severe penalties for hurting a cat. To kill a cat in the city of Venice was to condemn oneself to die within the year. Resident of the grandest of the Venetian palaces, the cat was associated with the noblest families of the city, even a doge, Fransesco Morosini, who would take along his cat, Dogaress, a brave female cat who was at ease on the prow of his warship, and in land battles she shared the command tent with her master.

Strays were fed in a daily ritual in the central parts of the city by the women of Venice who became known as 'mama gati' or 'Mama cats'. Since the eighteenth century the mama gati have been known to prepare the inimitable Cat Spaghetti for their hungry feline friends. The spaghetti was covered in a delicious sauce of mussels, garlic, dry white wine, tomato sauce, parsley and olive oil. Unsurprisingly, it was not only the cats who benefited from the pasta feasts. Humans also found it an irresistible recipe.

Just as cats inspired writers and artists, so they have been the companions of musicians. Cats are known to have been the inspiration for several great musicians. An impresario named Bisset, not to be confused with the composer Georges Bizet, produced a 'Cat's Opera' in London in 1758, in which a number of cats took part. Bisset trained his cats into choirs where they would meow and caterwaul to order.

Domenico Scarlatti (1685-1757) was one of the ten children of Alessandro Scarlatti, who was also a composer. Little is known about Scarlatti's private life. Although he was supposed to have been both gluttonous and a gambler, this is now doubted. What is certain is that he was a cat lover, and that his cat, Pulcinella, is remembered for her habit of walking up and down his open harpsichord. Rather than being irritated by this, Scarlatti was inspired and he wrote *The Cat Fugue* (Fugue in G Minor: L499) in which the music recalls the meowing tones of his feline companion. Scarlatti told how his cat 'would walk on the keys, going up and down from one end to the other. Sometimes he would pause longer on one note listening closely until the vibration ceased.'

Rossini produced the famous '*Duetto Buffo dei Due Gatti*' or 'The Buffo Duet of the Two Cats' in which the two female voices represent a quarrel between two cats.

Singers also have had adored cats as their companions. Usually, when cats died they were only remembered by their owners. However, Mrs Tofts, an eccentric opera singer of the late eighteenth century, left legacies to her twenty cats so that throughout their lives people would remember not only Mrs Tofts but the debt she owed and had repaid to her cats. Mrs Tofts apparently felt that the worst aspect of death was the wrench of parting with her cats. Peter Pindar, consecutively doctor, parson and doctor again, before becoming a writer, wrote:

> 'Nor Niobe mourned more for fourteen brats,
> Not Mrs Tofts to leave her twenty cats.'

Opposite: Winter Quarters by Paton and Allais, 1881. The cat's love of warm, snug spaces is well-documented across the ages.

Cats are more multi-talented than is supposed. Not only were there choirs of cats, some cats could be trained to perform in circuses, while others could become adept at fishing. Some strains of cat don't exhibit the fear of water that most display. Charles Darwin (1809-1882), naturalist and writer, was among those who have been intrigued by the ability of some cats to fish. In Turkey one breed of cat is predominantly a fish-eater and in Paris there must have been at least one seventeenth-century diving cat that made a name for itself. A street dating from this period named the 'rue du Chat qui pêche' commemorates its exploits.

While poets and artists sought to capture the essence of the cat in literature and painting, Charles Darwin (1809-1882) sought to analyze the natural behaviour of the cat. In *The Expression of Emotions* (1872) he wrote of the different emotions of the animal and how a cat's entire body posture, gait and movement expressed its moods. Darwin remarked that when a cat was feeling affectionate she would stand upright, with a slightly arched back, tail raised perpendicularly and ears erect, rubbing her cheeks and flanks against her master or mistress. Darwin observed that the need to rub something was so strong in cats that they might often be seen rubbing themselves against the legs of chairs or tables, or against door posts and that

> 'this manner of affection probably originated through association, as in the case of dogs, from the mother nursing and fondling her young; and perhaps from the young themselves loving each other and playing together'.

Another very different gesture observed by Darwin was the way cats, when pleased, alternately protrude their front paws, with separated toes, as if pushing against something, and sucking their toes. He maintained that both were derived from actions performed during the nursing period of a kitten. In terms of this kneading movement Darwin wrote: 'Kittens, puppies, young pigs and probably many other animals push with their fore-feet against the mammary glands of their mothers, to excite a freer secretion of milk, or to make it flow... It is very common with

Overleaf: White Cats Catching Goldfish, by Arthur Heyer (1872-1931). Cats are never more curious than when entranced at the sight of such irresistable yet unattainable prey.

young cats, and not at all rare with old cats of the common and Persian breeds, when comfortably lying on a warm shawl or other soft substance, to pound it quietly and alternately with their fore'feet; their toes being spread out and claws slightly protruded, precisely as when sucking their mother'.

'Why cats should show affection by rubbing so much more than dogs, though the latter delight in contact with their masters, and why cats only occasionally lick the hands of their friends, whilst dogs always do so, I cannot say. Cats cleanse themselves by licking their own coats more regularly than do dogs. On the other hand, their tongues seem less well fitted for the work than the longer and more flexible tongues of dogs'.

In addition Darwin noted that a contented cat also rolled a lot, both from side to side and also completely over, rolling onto its back to present its under surface 'for an all-round and much appreciated tickle'. A caressing hand may be licked or nibbled, depending on the cat's degree of exhilaration and kicks of varying strength administered. Reserved cats accept their tickles with little outward display, while the more demonstrative cat will swoon with pleasure, looking with melting eyes and drooling. A happy cat will frequently chase its tail.

In his studies of the cat, Darwin often drew comparisons between cat and dog. He writes 'Smiling and laughing are far less frequent in cats than in dogs even though they are capable of greater facial expression, unequalled, in fact, except by humans. Their more subtle and subdued humour seldom necessitates laughter. It is generally more of a gentle teasing nature, not boisterous, and can be directed at people, other cats or other animals. They usually show pleasure and amusement by a variety of facial expressions combined with body movements'.

By contrast, when terrified cats 'stand at full height, and arch their backs in a well-known and ridiculous fashion. They spit, hiss, or growl. The hair over the whole body, and especially on the tail, becomes erect.'

Chapter 8

VICTORIAN CATS & OWNERS
OF DISTINCTION

The cat's-meat man was one of the street traders in the bustling London of the first half of the nineteenth century. They vied with chestnut roasters, the French-onion sellers and paper boys and a host of other people selling their wares in the centre of the great city. In the poorer districts of the city the cats lives depended on the cat's-meat man. Many of his customers couldn't afford more than a ha'penny a day to feed their cat. If supplies failed and prices rose poverty was such that at a penny a day, or even every other day, the cats would starve. The street traders prided themselves on the number of times they had kept the alley cats going. The meat was horse meat,

Opposite: At Home: A Portrait by Walter Crane (1845-1915). A friend of William Morris, Crane is recognised as one of the greatest and most innovative of all children's books illustrators.

collected from the knacker's yard. At the beginning of the day the street trader would take the cheaper cuts at tuppence ha'penny a pound from the horse butcher, or smaller pieces sold on skewers at anything from a farthing to a penny each.

Until the advent of the car, London had traffic jams that now can only be visualized. The noise was horrendous, so loud that whenever someone was ill their friends or relatives scattered straw on the street outside their house to deaden the sound of the wheels on the stones in the roads. The hustle and bustle of horse-drawn transport could only be maintained because of the number of mews and stables that were scattered around the city. Inevitably, sooner or later the horses failed and became meat for cats and dogs. Wherever there were stables, even if it was only a shed sheltering the costermonger's donkey rather than well-appointed stalls and loose-boxes attached to the great houses in the West End, there would also be cats.

The cat's-meat man learnt where the cats were, who was responsible for them and who would be prepared to pay for his goods. The cats also recognized the sound of the trader's cart and came to know the time that it would arrive in their street. They were probably unable to recognise that the cat's-meat man, just as those in other trades, had their own uniform. According to Henry Mayhew (1812-1887), they traditionally wore a shiny hat, black plush waistcoat and sleeves, a blue apron, corduroy trousers, and a blue and white spotted handkerchief round the neck. The more flamboyant among them would wear two or three of these bright handkerchiefs, in a manner made popular by old Mr Brontë who wore multiple stocks.

There was at least one spinster in Early Victorian London who was a lavish patroness of cats in her neighbourhood and became established as one of its great characters. She was an African lady – there were far more people of African origin in London from Elizabethan times onwards than is now realised. She would buy as much as fourpence-worth of cat's meat a day, a generous gesture, for at the time a medical student would be expected to live on ninepence a day. The African lady would then climb up on to the roof of her house, and feed the cats who would rush over the neighbouring tiles to receive their ration. She insisted that her cats shouldn't be allowed to start their day hungry. If the cat's-meat man hadn't been in the street before ten o'clock in the morning she would seek him out in the shed that was the centre of his business. Daily, between ten and eleven o'clock, the mews of the hundreds of stray cats attracted to the spot were so ear-splitting, even terrible to hear, that those who lived nearby complained regularly, rather as today people complain about a pigeon feeder in their district.

If Charles Dickens (1812-1870) is to be believed it wasn't only kind humans who fed the cats, but also unkindly humans who fed them to their kith and kin. Dickens describes how one of the acquaintances of Sam Weller in *Pickwick Papers* was a pieman who could and did make pies out of anything, including cats.

Dickens describes the scene: "'What a number o' cats you keep, Mr Brooks", says I, when I'd got intimate with him. "Ah," says he, "I do – a good many" says he. "You must be very fond of cats," says I. "Other people is," says he, winkin' at me – "Why, what do you mean?" says I. "Mean?" says he. "That I'll never be a party to the combination o' the butchers to keep up the prices o' meat," says he. "Mr Weller," says he, squeezing my hand very hard and vispering in my ear, "don't mention this again, but it's the seasonin' as does it. They're all made o' them noble animals," says he, a-pointin' to a very nice little tabby kitten, "I seasons 'em for beefsteak, weal or kidney, 'cordin to the demand.'"

By the time that Henry Mayhew wrote about London, the use of cat meat in pies, seasoned or not,

The 1884 Crystal Palace Cat Show, taken from *The Illustrated Sporting and Dramatic News* 1883.

Kate Nickleby sitting to Miss La Creevy, *Nicholas Nickleby*, by
Charles Dickens.

was over. He states categorically that the pies sold in the London streets were 'made of beef or mutton'.

Dickens elsewhere gives us an account of a black cat that served as a witch's familiar in *Dombey and Son*. This old cat belonged to what was then referred to as a child-queller, but today would be known as a foster parent. Mrs Pipchin was notorious. She kept an infant boarding house at Brighton where Paul Dombey was sent for the benefit of sea-air. This cat 'generally lay coiled up upon the centre foot of the fender, purring egotistically and winking at the fire until the contracted pupils of his eyes were like two notes of admiration. The good old lady might have been – not to record it disrespectfully – a witch and Paul and the cat her two familiars, as they all sat by the fire together. It would have been quite in keeping with the appearance of the party if they had all sprung up the chimney in a high wind one night and never been heard of any more.'

'This, however,' adds Dickens gravely, 'never came to pass.' As was the case with most of Dickens' characters, the appearance and behaviour of Mrs Pipchin was based on that of a real person who had figured in Dickens' life. Mrs Pipchin was in reality Mrs Roylance, an elderly woman living in reduced circumstances with whom a youthful Charles lodged for a time in Camden Town. This was when his family were incarcerated in the debtor's prison at Mashalsea, and he himself was working in the rat-infested warehouse by Hungerford Stairs. It was owned by his wife's relations, but it didn't spare him the job of pasting wrappings and labels on Warren's blacking.

Dickens used a certain amount of artistic license in describing Mrs Roylance's house in Camden. The cottage where he lodged bore little resemblance to the 'ogress's castle' at Brighton. The 'infantine boarding-house' while he was there had impecunious lodgers rather than children. The Roylance enterprise was of what Mrs Chick described as 'an exceedingly limited and particular scale'. However, there is no doubt that Dickens' account of her black cat was taken from life.

At Dover Miss Betsy Trotwood had for her companions, when her nephew David Copperfield startled her by his sudden appearance, one cat and two canaries. All these pets were still in being when she and Mr Dick turned up so unexpectedly at David's lodgings in Buckingham Street, Strand, where, to his amazement, he found his aunt 'sitting on a quantity of luggage with her two birds before her and her cat on her knee, like a female Robinson Crusoe, drinking tea'.

A lank and meagre cat shared with the equally lank and meagre Marchioness the cellar in Bevis Marks where Dick Swiveller began his transformation from a shabby, cheeky young clerk into the most delightful and charming man in *The Old Curiosity Shop*.

Dickens gives no impression that he was a great cat lover, but even if he was slightly antipathetic to them there is no evidence that he actively disliked them. Years later his approach to cats changed. Dickens was a great family man and he was tolerant of his daughter Mamie's cat, Williamina. Williamina gave birth to kittens in the kitchen of Charles Dickens' house and carried them one by one into his study. Mamie took her kittens away but Williamina found them and brought them and laid them at Dickens' feet. Charles Dickens let Mamie keep one kitten, but this kitten grew up to become his pet and he named her 'The Master's Cat'.

The ancient Egyptian, Greek and early Roman agricultural experts had noted that the cat's ability to deal with mice improved the subsequent grain harvest. Dickens made a similar observation. He drew farmers' attention to a similar effect that the presence of cats in the field had on the amount of purple clover in a crop, and hence the quality of the hay and the subsequent

fertility of the field. He had been interested to observe that the quality of the clover depended on the number of cats that prowled around the fields. The chain of causation is thus unwound. The more cats, the fewer field-mice; the fewer field-mice, the more bumble-bees; the more bumble-bees, the more abundant the purple clover fertilized by them – and, consequently, the more contented the live-stock which feed upon the flowers.

Charles Dickens was famous as a dog lover and was accustomed to walk the dogs rather as a dog walker now takes her charges through a London park. Sir Walter Scott (1771-1832) also was famed for his love of dogs, but in general writers were known for their preference for cats. There are many examples of a natural affinity between writers and cats. Writers tend to be self-contained, rather solitary people, who find it difficult to share their emotions readily, or even to be recipients of the boisterous love that a dog may display. Cats suit the personality of the writer better.

Opposite: An early nineteenth century photograph depicts a cat's welcome home.

Thackeray (1811-1868), whose own domestic life was blighted by his wife's ill-health, sought solace in casual relationships. He also had a favourite cat, Louisa, who lived a favoured life as she was allowed to snuggle under his waistcoat and doze throughout the afternoon. Louisa was fed on the best fish that London had to offer. Not for her oysters that were at this time the equivalent of fish and chips, but the fish from Thackeray's breakfast plate. When he had to get on with his life and writing he didn't shoo her roughly away, but gathered her up gently and put her outside the door. His family noticed how attached he had become to Louisa and his daughter described in one of her letters to Mrs Baxter in 1861 that Papa had become passionately attached to a little cat. His family seemed to have inherited his love of cats and there is a record that later they fed an army of stray cats. Daily they laid out a row of saucers under their medlar tree and along the terrace, in front of Thackeray's study.

Opposite: Kitten and Ball of Wool, 1866, by the Japanese artist Murata Kokudu. By the nineteenth century the cat featured in many paintings in a much more sympathetic and affectionate light, appreciated for its playful and endearing qualities.

The cats were named after characters in Dickens' novels. The Thackerays tried to make the name appropriate, so that Nicholas Nickleby was given to 'a huge grey tabby' and Barnaby Rudge was inadequate and weak.

It wasn't only British writers who were keen cat collectors. Alexandre Dumas (1802-1870) was so fond of his cats that he formed a Feline Defence League and lost no time in recruiting fellow cat lovers and authors to its ranks. Guy de Maupassant, Anatole France and Charles Baudelaire were all cat lovers and all joined the Defence League.

An interesting account of the second sight of cats is told about Mysouff, Dumas' favourite cat and so loved by his owner that much later, after the death of his beloved companion, Dumas gave another later cat the same name. Dumas lived with his mother in the rue de l'Ouest in Paris. His office was in the rue St Honoré, which was at least a mile from his mother's house. Mysouff accompanied Dumas for part of the walk to the office and then turned round at exactly the same place each day and went home. In the evening he would get up from his fireside seat. Mrs Dumas senior would open the door for Mysouff who would set off back to the office. When he reached the place where he had left his master that morning he would wait patiently for him. Sometimes Dumas had another appointment in the evening, or would work late. On these occasions he wouldn't leave his fireside seat and nothing would entice him to start on what he knew, by whatever means, would be a fruitless walk. So accurate was Mysouff at knowing whether his master had an unexpected other engagement that the mistress of the house knew whether she should cook dinner for him.

When Mysouff the second, successor to the original Mysouff, was discovered to have eaten Dumas' collection of exotic birds he gave the cat a trial before his dinner guests. One acted in the animal's defence, arguing that the aviary door had been opened by a monkey. The verdict agreed upon was that the poor cat must serve five years' incarceration in the company of the monkeys. However, Dumas was not a wealthy man and the monkeys were sold soon after, thus liberating the wretched feline.

Collette (1873-1954), who always had a creative imagination, wrote a series of fanciful conversations between her grey angora, Kiki-la Doucette, and Toby, her French bulldog. The resulting book was so successful that it was even translated into English and in the United Kingdom it was sold under the title *Barks and Purrs*. One of her other cat stories was a

tribute to her cat, Saha. She used the same name in her book, *La Chatte,* in which the heroine was a gorgeous Russian Blue female. The only problem was that the cat was so beautiful that a young man met it and then preferred it to his own bride. An earlier writer, George Sand (1804-1876), also attributed almost human qualities to Minou, her cat, and at breakfast time the two of them shared the same plate.

Théophile Gautier (1811-1872) was obsessed by his cats and wrote about them in his book *La Ménagerie Intime.* There was Madame Théophile, a red and white cat who was so called because she liked to share her master's bed. Madame Théophile was known for her strong dislike of singing and high notes would send her to hide beneath the bed. There was also Childebrand, a striped black and tan who looked like a tiger, and a white cat named Don Pierrot de Navarre who would watch his master's pen as he wrote. Another white cat belonging to Gautier was Seraphita. He was so enamoured of this feline companion, that he wrote of her 'never did a cat more amply justify a poetic name'.

Opposite: Charles van den Eyken's portrait of a kitten, c. 1895. A cat will delight in exploring and form their reputation for curiosity from kittenhood.

Seraphita was just as devoted to her master. Gautier wrote that they would 'sit on a cushion for hours together' and that she would follow him with her eyes 'in a rapture of attention, sights invisible to mere mortals. Caresses were agreeable to her, but she would return them ... only in the case of those people she favoured with her rare esteem.' Seraphita, like many cats, was fond of luxury. 'It was ... upon the handsomest, most comfortable chair, or the rug that would best show off her snowy fur, that she would be found.' A great beauty, she would smooth her glossy coat each morning and lick every bit of her fur with her pink tongue until it shone like new silver. A cat among cats, she had an aura of aristocracy suggested by her elegance, and among her own people she was a duchess at least, delighting even in perfumes and even biting scented handkerchiefs and walking about among the scent bottles on the dressing table. Don Pierrot de Navarre and Seraphita had three kittens who were named after characters in Victor Hugo's *Les Miserables*, Enjoras, Gavroche and Eponine, who would sit at the dinner table with Gautier for their supper.

In *The Paradise of Cats* Emile Zola (1814-1902) tells of a two-year-old Angora cat bequeathed to him by one of his aunts. The fat cat was idolized and had every comfort afforded to him — a feather pillow at the bottom of a cupboard and good quality meat to eat. Jealous of the apparent freedom of other cats who live a life on the tiles, the Angora escaped, but in due course returned to the good life he had left behind.

Zola's contemporary Charles Baudelaire (1821-1867) was so obsessed by cats that he caused outrage and uproar on several occasions, expressing a preference for the company of his feline friends to humans. One newspaper article of the time states that: 'It has become the fashion in the society formed by Baudelaire and his companions to make too much of cats… Baudelaire, going for the first time to a house, and on business, is uneasy and restless until he has seen the household cat. But when he sees it he takes it up, kisses and strokes it, and is so completely occupied with it that he makes no answer to anything that is said of him. People stare at this breech of good manners.'

Writers often displayed their love of the cat by allowing them to rest on their shoulder, as did Edgar Allen Poe (1809-1849), but they would also project their feline experiences on to the actions of the characters in their books. One cat, Foss, the beloved tom cat belonging to Edward Lear (1812-1888), Victorian artist and humorist, achieved fame and

Edward Lear's striped tom-cat, Foss, immortalised by his owner's delightful sketches. When Lear moved house when Foss was elderly, he had a new house built with the same layout as the old one, so that Foss would know his way around.

immortality through the sketches of his master. Cartoons of Foss in different heraldic positions such as rampant, couchant, passant and regardant were published by Lear in a collection of drawings under the title *The Heraldic Blazon of Foss the Cat*. Foss had been a member of the Lear family since 1873. When just a small kitten his tail was removed by a servant named Georgio, who believed this would prevent the animal from straying. When Foss died in 1887, the elderly Lear insisted on a full burial service and a grave marked by a large tombstone incorrectly stating the cat's age as being thirty-one. In fact, Foss was just fourteen and Lear survived him by just two months.

One imaginary small girl of Victorian literature who was devoted to cats was Alice from *Alice in Wonderland*. Lewis Carroll (1832-1898), like birthday-card artists down the ages, felt that no household which included a small girl was complete unless there was a cat or kitten to round off the picture. Alice's cat in the book rather than in real life in Oxford was called Dinah. Dinah was present at many of Alice's adventures in Wonderland. Alice was so attached to her that even when mysterious disasters came upon them Alice's first thought was for Dinah. 'Dinah'll miss me very much to-night, I should think. I hope they'll remember her saucer of milk at tea-time. Dinah my dear, I wish you were down here with me!' Readers of *Alice in Wonderland* are able to plot some of the life of Dinah. In *Alice through the Looking Glass* Dinah eventually had kittens, including one black and one white.

One of Lewis Carroll's cats has not only lived in literature, but has become part of the English language. The Cheshire Cat that had figured in a little-known proverb became immortal after it had such a prominent role in *Alice in Wonderland*. The cat is now forever remembered sitting either by the kitchen fire of the

The famous Cheshire Cat, as illustrated by John Tenniel in the first edition of *Alice in Wonderland*, by Lewis Carroll (1866).

Ugly Duchess or straddled like a leopard on the bough of a tree just above Alice's head. In the past, before Lewis Carroll had made the Cheshire Cat famous, its chief call to fame had been as a mould in which Cheshire cheese was at one time made. It was possible, according to Brewer's *Dictionary of Phrase and Fable*, to buy Cheshire cheese not in a bland round, but in the shape of a grinning face of a cat.

Although cats are the faithful companions of people of all ages and both sexes, they are frequently pictured with young girls and elderly women. If Alice was the archetypal girl to be a cat lover, Mrs Forrester's cat is immortalized in Elizabeth Gaskell's (1810-1865) *Cranford*. Although Mrs Forrester had made a good marriage and had been a dignified widow, it was her cat that had set her apart from the rest of the elderly ladies of her circle. This cat was always admirably turned out and usually wore a very fine lace collar; Mrs Forrester was proud to tell her friend Lady Glenmire, that she washed herself in milk.

A small girl who must have lived at about the same time as *Alice in Wonderland* was written once went to stay with one of her relatives in a house in Hampstead. The small girl was the daughter of the poet Arthur Hugh Clough (1819–1861), and her hostess was none other than Miss Florence Nightingale (1820–1910). There is still a description of this visit in her journal and she describes the scene in her bedroom when the cats received their young visitor.

It was in the same year that Florence's father, employing every wile he could think of to tempt her back to her old home, and to him, tried to soften her resistance by describing the activities of the favourite cats she had left behind. A year later one of her Hampstead cats would kiss her eyelids and, when necessary, lick the tears off her cheeks. More than thirty years later she made this characteristic promise: 'I learn the lesson of life from a little kitten of mine, one of two. The old cat comes in and says, very cross, 'I didn't ask you in here. I like to have my Missis to myself.' The bigger and handsomer kitten runs away; but the little one *stands her ground*: and when the old enemy comes near enough kisses his nose and makes the peace. That is the lesson of life; to kiss one's enemy's nose always standing one's ground.' Florence Nightingale, the 'Lady of the Lamp', was a determined campaigner so she was frequently visited by the famous men of her time. Although she claimed to place a kiss on the cheeks of eminent persons whom she met, so fierce was her campaigning they may have felt that it was more akin to a scratch from one of their cats rather than an affectionate kiss.

Florence Nightingale was able to describe the individual characteristics of all sixty of her cats and was equally attached to all of them. If she had to travel they all went too, every one of them. The cats were large and Persian and had a gravitas about them that suited their names. Each was named after one of the statesmen of the day, and Florence being both well-travelled and well-versed in politics, the names were those of foreign statesmen as well as those of British ones, and of Liberals as well as Conservatives.

'Beware', said Voltaire once, 'of a woman who does not like cats.' Florence Nightingale would have met with his approval. Another eminent Victorian who was just as besotted with cats as Florence Nightingale was Christina Rossetti. 'The Jael,' as Swinburne called her, 'who led the Pre-Raphaelite hosts to victory', was a lover of all animals, of which cats were only one.

Throughout her life Christina Rossetti (1830-1894) was attracted by any cat that was small, soft and defenseless. In her later life she extended the age range of her cats and simultaneously took comfort from the company of a rough, tough tom cat as well as a small kitten, such as she had nurtured in her earlier years.

The two would play together in her Bloomsbury drawing room and many of her interests revolved around her two cats. Almost up until her death she was writing to William Michael, her brother, and described their antics and the attention she paid to them. 'I have turned doctor myself! Rubbing a kitten who appears weak, to say the least of it, in the hindlegs with camphorated oil. Yesterday I flattered myself that the treatment gave some promise of amendment. Such a pretty kitten, with such a rich fur.'

Rossetti's admirer, Algernon Swinburne (1837-1909), also had a cat, but so far as we know his cat and her cats never met. If they had it is quite probable that Swinburne's would not have cared for Rossetti's alley cat, for Swinburne's cat had been described by his master as a 'stately, kindly, lordly friend', not the sort of cat to either hobnob with a rough, tough tom nor enjoy friendly games with a small kitten.

Across the Atlantic Samuel Langhorne Clemens better known as Mark Twain (1835-1910), American writer and humorist, described the cat of Dick Baker, a gold miner. Dick Baker owned Tom Quartz, a cat that although never caught a rat in his life, was a natural-born prospector. They tramped the hills together. The cat would look around when they reached any possible site and if it didn't rise to Tom Quartz's expectations, they would wander back to the camp. On other occasions he would just stay and lie on the ground until Dick Baker had washed the first pan. Invariably Tom Quartz would inspect the residue and if there was gold in it, he wandered away satisfied. The cat was Dick Baker's constant companion for eight years, and on one occasion even survived being blown up when the miners unwittingly lit the fuse without realising that the cat was marking out the spot where he had suspected that gold lay. Astonishingly he recovered, although battered. After this adventure he would be off as fast as he could, whenever he saw preparations being made to the light a fuse.

Twain was an ardent cat lover and wrote that 'a house without a cat, a well-fed, well-petted and properly revered cat, may be a perfect house, perhaps, but how can it prove its title?' All of Twain's cats sported exotic names, such as Zoroaster, Blatherskite and Sour Mash, as he believed that this would assist the children in long pronunciation of difficult words.

In nineteenth-century England, Thomas Hardy (1840-1928) was heartbroken when his cat died. He even wrote an obituary poem to it. Many years later when he was elderly he was given a beautiful grey

Persian with amber eyes, whom he named Cobby. It is said that Cobby remained at Hardy's side until Hardy's death in 1928 when Cobby mysteriously disappeared.

There were many musicians from the period who were great admirers of cats. The Russian composer Alexander Borodin (1833-1887) adored cats and he and his wife owned a large number of them. Rimsky-Korsakoff (1844-1908) even wrote an account showing his great surprise at how they would be allowed to walk across the dinner table and even eat off the plates. Johannes Brahms (1833-1897) could not have taken a more different view of the feline species. He hated cats so intensely that he would shoot them with arrows shot from a bow given him by Antonín Dvorák (1841-1904). Richard Wagner (1813-1883) wrote that 'after spearing the poor brutes, he reeled them into his room after the manner of a trout fisher. Then he eagerly listened to the expiring groans of his victims and carefully jotted down in his notebook there antemortem remarks'.

Opposite: The French artist Théophile Steinlen (1859-1923) observed in detail the nuances of cat behaviour and posture in many sketches and studies created over a number of years.

'Puss in Perplexity'

Many famous artists became well known for their depictions of the cat in their paintings. In the early Victorian age Gottfried Mind (1768-1814), a hunchback from Berne in Switzerland painted hundreds of cats and was dubbed the 'Raphael of Cats'.

Opposite: 'Tinkie', by South African-born artist Derold Page. Although the black cat was reviled for centuries because of its association with witchcraft, over the ages the white cat has enjoyed greater popularity as it became a symbol of good fortune and prosperity

Chapter 9

WORKING CATS,
CATS OF LUXURY & DECADENCE
IN MODERN TIMES

The tradition of ecclesiastical sets is as much alive now as it was in medieval times and there are many church and cathedral cats thriving among the precincts and cloisters. The convent of St Nicholas of the Cats in Cyprus is home to over two hundred cats, most of which are feral but fed by the nuns. Legend has it the cats have been at the convent since 328AD when St Helena of the Cross, mother of Constantine the Great, was at Akrotiri on the south coast. The long association with cats has led to the Cape being known as the 'Cape Gata', or 'Cape of Cats'.

St Helena's visit came after a great drought had led to a proliferation of snakes and many people living there had died of snake bites. St Helena persuaded her

Opposite: Cat nestling in the garden with a butterly, 1990, by Lynette Hemmant.

son to take the necessary steps to control the snake menace. He arranged for a group of cats to be brought from Egypt to destroy them. The cats bred almost as quickly as the snakes had done and, according to the legend, in no time at all more than one thousand cats were stalking the snakes. These cats prospered well into the Middle Ages and reference to them in 1484 is found in the records of one Venetian monk. The monk commented that there were still many snakes but even more cats that waged war against them. The war wasn't all one-sided and some cats bore evidence of their battles with the venomous reptiles, having lost an ear or being blinded.

By 1580, the monks living in the monastery were presented the surrounding land on condition they would feed at least one hundred cats every morning and evening. The monks willingly carried out their duty to the cats until the monastery fell into ruin in the sixteenth century. Many of the cats starved to death. In time, the building was restored to provide a new sanctuary for the descendants of the ancient cats. Within the last twenty years the cats had multiplied to such an extent that visitors complained that over-population was resulting in their poor condition. The local WSPA [World Society for the Protection of Animals] provided more food and

A Cat in the Window of a Cottage by the Newcastle-born
Victorian oil painter and wood carver Ralph Hedley (1851-
1913). The cat's closed eyes indicate he is completely relaxed
and content enjoying the sun from his place on the sill.

neutered many of the females. Nowadays, the cats are well looked after and their population is well controlled.

Over the centuries the Church provided less and less administration functions but the cats weren't doomed. The new government offices and institutions that superseded some of the Church's functions had also need of vermin operatives. Working cats are valued as mousers in museums, government institutions and workplaces.

Mike (1908-1929) was the cat at the British Museum in London for twenty years. Black Jack, the previous museum cat dropped Mike the kitten at the feet of the Keeper of Egyptian cat mummies. Mike rewarded his benefactors, for his skills were not limited to catching mice, he also won fame for his ability to catch pigeons. Workers at the museum looked after Mike, even during the First World War when they made sure he was well fed. Wallis Budge, the famous Egyptologist wrote that Mike 'preferred sole to whiting and whiting to haddock, and sardines to herring, for cod he had no use whatsoever'.

Working cats have also been employed in the Post Office, where since 1866 their duties have been to protect the sacks of letters from rats and mice. In 1868 a large number of money orders were nibbled by mice and in the summer the department manager

US Marine Frank Praytor adopted an orphaned kitten, naming her 'Miss Hap' because she was 'born in the wrong place at the wrong time'.

requested that the number of cats should be increased to three to control the problem. The Secretary of the Post Office agreed and, after a series of negotiations, awarded the sum of one shilling per week for their wages. The Secretary stipulated that if they failed in their task the allowance would be reduced and that under no circumstances were the cats to be overfed. A hundred years later the amount had increased to ten shillings and by the 1980s the cats' salary had increased to £2 a week. By then over 25,000 Post Office cats were officially employed.

In the early years of the Post Office and during both world wars it was common to send food parcels through the post, encouraging a boom in the rat population. Cats were the perfect solution to a tricky problem, since it was thought that scattering rat poison among the packages would prove a danger if it contaminated the post and was accidentally eaten by those receiving it. Traps were considered a poor alternative and were abandoned because of the risk to the many workers handling and sorting the mail.

The entertainment world, too, has benefited from the skills of the cat. For more than five hundred years no theatre has been complete without its cat. One modern-day mouser employed at the Gielgud Theatre

Lait pur de la Vingeanne Stérilisé

guillot frères
Montigny sur Vingeanne
Côte d'Or

Steinlen

Lithograph from the '*Les Maitre de L'Affiches*' series by Théophile Alexandre Steinlen (1859–1923). He created many Art Nouveau illustrations and advertisements that often featured the cats that he loved.

217

was Beerbohm, named after Herbert Beerbohm Tree, the manager of Her Majesty's Theatre. Beerbohm began his mousing career at that theatre at an early age, and in time grew into a large tabby. His skills were in demand and in the md-1970s he was transferred by agreement to the Gielgud Theatre. There he could often be seen wandering across the stage during the middle of a performance, thereby upstaging all the actors. Beerbohm kept his consorting to the world of theatre, his chosen companion was Fleur, the female cat from the Lyric Theatre, a short distance away.

In Pittsburgh, in the late nineteenth century, cats were bred in large refrigeration plants. 'Refrigerator cats', as they were known, were developed to survive at the low temperatures of the factories and to catch the rats that were invading stores of food kept there. The cats were known to have long fur, thick tails and tufted ears and to look a little like the Canadian Lynx that survives in North America's harshest temperatures.

Cats had played a war-winning role for the ancient Persians when they invaded Egypt; two and a half thousand years later they were still an essential part of barrack life. In the First World War their role was crucial. Rats were one of the horrors that everybody who had served in the trenches never forgot. To counter the problem the British Government enlisted five hundred cats to patrol the trenches. Their sensitivity to poison gas also became important to the troops. If a cat collapsed and died, it indicated trouble for the soldiers.

The highly tuned senses of the cat were valued through the Second World War and beyond. In 1968 a platoon of military guide cats was shipped to Vietnam as field guides during night patrols in the jungle. Desmond Morris (1928-) reports that the only consolation to be gained from this bizarre experiment was its effect on the Viet Cong. It is said that when they heard of this new secret weapon several of them died laughing.

There are several well-documented stories of cats of heroism and adventure during wartime. During the Blitz in London, a cat known as Bomber apparently knew the difference between the engine sounds of approaching British and German planes and could hear them before his human companions. As a result he was used as a warning system for the troops. During the Blitz an unnamed cat proved a courageous and resourceful mother. An inscription in one of the City churches, since taken down, told her story: 'Shielding her kitten in a sort of recess in the house (a spot she selected only three days before the tragedies occurred), she sat the whole frightful night of bombing and fire, guarding her little kitten. The roofs and masonry exploded, the whole house lazed, four floors fell through in front of her. Fire and ruin all around her. Yet she stayed calm and steadfast and waited for help. We rescued her in the early morning while the place was still burning, and by the mercy of Almighty God she and her kitten were not only saved, but unhurt.'

Cats were put to good use by the Navy as rat catchers and as lucky mascots. The most famous was Oscar. Oscar began as the mascot of the German battleship Bismarck. When the Bismarck sank in 1941 Oscar was spotted swimming in the wreckage and was fished out by a British naval officer. Oscar was taken on board the HMS Cossack and soon settled in. Five months later the Cossack was also sunk and once again Oscar survived. This time he was rescued by the crew of the Ark Royal and this became his home. When in due course the Ark Royal was attacked by a German U-boat Oscar was rescued yet again. The naval authorities decided that Oscar had done his bit for the Navy and deserved some peace and quiet. He retired from the sea to spend the rest of his days happily in a sailor's home.

One remarkable cat named Mourka is famous for his bravery and help during the Second World War when he was used to carry messages during the siege of

Cats were popular mascots for soldiers fighting on the fronts during the Second World War.

Stalingrad in 1942. Mourka knew the kitchens were located beside the house to which the messages needed to be taken and hence he was always inspired in his brave rush through the enemy's territory. Mourka's heroism became well known and there were stories about him in many newspapers. One article in *The Times* revered him with the words 'whether for cat or man there can be no higher praise'.

British cats saw active service in the air as well as at sea and on land. Wing Commander Guy Gibson, VC, the famous dam buster of the Second World War, was often kept company on his wartime missions by Windy, his cat.

Although some cats have become attached to famous buildings and other institutions in both peace and war, far more have become the close companions of famous people. The film star James Mason was a great cat lover. He owned many cats, mostly Siamese. He and his wife took several with them when they travelled from England to New York in the 1940s.

Many other Hollywood legends also doted on their cats. Among them were Fred Astaire, Lucille Ball, Charlie Chaplin, Katherine Hepburn, Charles Laughton and Elizabeth Taylor. Brigitte Bardot is well known for her love of animals and for having founded

One of the iconic Steinlen posters for Le Chat Noir cabaret.

Bridget Bardot, *La Mariee est trop belle*, (1956) is a famous cat lover. Her foundation, the Mare Azou, has rescued over two hundred cats.

a shelter for them in St Tropez, France. Away from the shelter, in her own home, she looks after a further fifty stray cats.

Cats lived in theatres and were the companions of actors, but their contact with the stage didn't end there. A white cat named Arthur became a TV star in his own right in the 1960s and seventies. He appeared in TV adverts publicising a wide range of products from Spillers cat food to T-shirts. He even has his autobiography published, ghosted by John Montgomery.

Arthur had the remarkable ability to eat food out of a tin with his paw. The adverts were so successful that Spillers bought him for a large sum of money. The transaction became the subject of a High Court custody battle between Spillers and his former owner. On the first day of the hearing Arthur went missing and the owner pleaded that the cat would be found in the Russian Embassy. He was jailed for contempt of court. A couple of weeks later Arthur reappeared and his former owner unsuccessfully sought damages from Spillers. Arthur died in 1976 aged sixteen. It would be another decade before Arthur could be replaced.

Eventually, animal trainer Ann Head spotted a cat named Snowy in a London animal shelter where he was suffering badly from malnutrition and a cold. She took him in and slowly he recovered. Once better he began a successful career for Spillers. Snowy, like Arthur, was able to eat food out of the tin with his paw.

In the United States another cat achieved equal fame and fortune from a television career. Morris was discovered in a Chicago animal shelter in 1968. Although named Lucky when he was found, this large ginger tom soon assumed the name of Morris, the cat food he advertised. Morris was a fussy eater but had a placid, docile temperament, which proved a winning formula with the producers as well as the American public.

Morris starred in forty commercials in the years that followed and enjoyed a Hollywood celebrity lifestyle. He was driven around in a limousine, appeared on talk shows and received fan letters from all over the world. He even dined at the White House and used a litter tray designed by Louis Vuitton. Millions mourned his death in 1978. It proved as difficult to replace Morris as it had been to find a successor for Arthur. Morris the Second, when found two years later, looked identical to Morris the First. Like his namesake he soon became famous and was also revered enough to have a book written about him. The highlight of his career came in 1988 when he was elected as a presidential candidate because he was so

Cat, 1947, an ink drawing by the Japanese painter and
engraver Tsugouharu Leonard Foujita, otherwise known as
Fujita (1886-1968). Foujita was a friend of Picasso and
Matisse. All three were great cat lovers and each captured
their beloved felines in their art.

famous and adored. However, his political career was short-lived and he was narrowly beaten to office.

Orangey was another cat that achieved fame and fortune in the media. Orangey was a ginger cat who starred in films; off-camera he became notorious for his unpredictable temper. Starring as 'Cat', in *Breakfast at Tiffany's* in 1961 with Audrey Hepburn, Orangey's fiery temperament made it necessary for him to have doubles in some of the scenes. He had previously appeared in *Rhubarb* (1951) in which he played a lucky cat that inherits a vast sum from his owner. During the filming of *Rhubarb*, Orangey proved so ratty and uncooperative that his human co-star Ray Milland was persuaded to have meat paste and cat nip rubbed on him, so that a better relationship could be established. Orangey's mood swings did not hamper his ultimate success and popularity and he twice won a Patsy (the Oscar of the animal world) before he died in 1963.

There have been several cartoon cats that have achieved great success and popularity. Felix was introduced by Paramount in the early twentieth century and appeared in hundreds of animated films, starring in the first talkie cartoon, well before Mickey Mouse. Felix was the epitome of a modern hero – brave, clever and resourceful – and his honourable character was designed to counter any lingering hostility towards cats inherited from their past association with witchcraft.

Following on from Felix's huge success MGM produced Tom and Jerry in 1939. These characters were created by Fred Quimby, William Hanna and Joseph Barbera. Tom and Jerry went on to receive seven Oscars during its eighteen years of success. Not to be outdone, Warner Brothers in 1945 launched its rival,

A sketch by actor James Mason of one of his Siamese cats named Sadie or Flower-face. The actor took his cats with him on film shoots and when travelling.

Marlon Brando loved cats both on and off set, as seen here in one famous scene from *The Godfather*.

Sylvester, in *Life with Feathers*. Sylvester was a black and white cat with a large ruff of white fur around his collar. Sylvester co-starred with Tweety Pie, a chubby canary in a cage who outsmarted the cat's attempts to devour the bird at every opportunity. Sylvester had a unique voice acted by Mel Blanc. Sylvester's speech impediment gave rise to the immortal catch phrase 'I tort I taw a puddy tat a-creeping up on me'.

Another cartoon cat was created in 1961 by Hanna Barbera for ABC. Top Cat, the hero, was known as TC to his friends and was a street-wise alley cat based on Sergeant Bilko. Top Cat lived in an old dustbin in Manhattan.

Robert Crumb invented Fritz, another famous cartoon cat, in 1965. Fritz caused much controversy when he swore and undertook a range of sexual adventures, yet he acquired a massive following during the 1960s. In 1971 he was relaunched amid further outrage. His work became the first ever x-rated cartoon. It was not a success and soon Fritz was overtaken by other cartoon cats such as Garfield. These appealed to a much wider audience. Garfield's charm ensured he became an instant hit when he was launched in 1977 and he was soon the subject of strip cartoons in hundreds of newspapers across the world.

The pampered lifestyle of Orangey and Morris was

not soley the domaine of the feline screen star. An Arabian Sheikh named Mohammad Al Fassi maintained about a hundred pet cats in his Florida mansion. A staff of nine, including a personal vet, were retained to care for the cats who lived in a suite of seven large rooms that had been set aside especially for them.

Working cats have enjoyed luxury lifestyles in high places other than in the media, although the nature of their work has been very different. At No 10 Downing Street, cats have been used to control the rat and mice population. One famous large black and white cat named Wilberforce outstayed several Prime Ministers, including Edward Heath, Harold Wilson, James Callaghan and Margaret Thatcher. Wilberforce was rescued as a kitten in 1973 and had been living at the RSPCA in Hounslow. Named by the caretaker of No 10 on account of a bust there of William Wilberforce, this cat waged a great war against the Downing Street mice. After thirteen years' service at No 10 Wilberforce retired to the country and died two years later on

Opposite: A poster of the film *Breakfast at Tiffanys*, starring Orangey the cat (and Audrey Hepburn).

This photo taken in 1952 shows then Prime Minister
Sir Winston Churchill meeting a new supporter at a visit to
Liverpool Street station.

19 May 1988. He was honoured by several obituaries that lamented the passing of the best mouser in Britain.

Winston Churchill (1874-1965) was a great lover of cats. Churchill reserved a special chair for his cat, Nelson, a black cat, in the Cabinet Room and another at the No 10 dining table. During the Second World War Nelson shared Churchill's bed, acting as a hot water bottle. Nelson was not the only cat to be doted on by the Prime Minister. Others were Bob, who would wait for Churchill on the steps on No. 10 and Mr Cat, a stray kitten who had turned up at No. 10. Margate, who was so named because he had appeared just after Churchill had made a speech in the town of Margate. Jock was a ginger tom who had been given to Churchill on his 88th birthday in 1962 by Sir John Colville.

Wilberforce's successor at No. 10 was Humphrey, named after the civil servant in the popular television series, *Yes Minister*. Humphrey arrived in Downing St and soon made himself indispensable. The security guards fed him at night and civil servants took on the task during the day. The civil servants complained: 'Despite being tried on just about every other brand of food, he will only eat Whiskas.' Indeed, if he didn't get the brand, Humphrey would go on hunger strike. His greatest moment was when the BBC came to film him, and Humphrey gave a very good imitation of a starving cat. 'Even the BBC, when filming him recently, commented on whether he was ill,' say Downing St records. At the arrival of Cherie Blair, who is allergic to cats, Humphrey was given a new home in the country.

Cats have graced the corridors of power on both sides of the Atlantic. Abraham Lincoln (1809-1865) discovered three orphan kittens during the Civil War on his visit to General Grant's headquarters. Fearing they would die of cold, he rescued them and they became part of the family along with Tabby, the pet of Lincoln's son Tad. Smoky was a wild Bobcat captured and given as a gift to President Calvin Coolidge (1872-1933). Smoky was quickly removed to a zoo for safekeeping. The next White House cat to become well known was a Siamese named Siam. Siam was a gift from the American Consul in Bangkok to Lucy Heyes, wife of President Hayes. Sadly Siam fell ill soon after her arrival in the States and died.

Theodore Roosevelt (1858-1919) owned a famous White House cat named Slippers. Slippers was a grey tabby with six toes. Slippers would disappear for days, coming and going as he pleased. On one occasion in 1906 he forced an entire procession of White House dinner guests to make a detour. He lay on the carpet

Vladimir Lenin was a renowned cat lover.

in the middle of the corridor between the State Dining Room and the East Room and refused to move for the President or his guests. Tom Quartz, named after Mark Twain's fictional cat, was another cat belonging to Roosevelt. Though small in stature, Tom Quartz would taunt and terrorize the black terrier belonging to the President's youngest son, Quentin.

John F. Kennedy (1917-1963) had Tom Kitten, who officially belonged to his daughter Caroline. Jimmy Carter (1924-) had Misty Malarky Ying Yang; again the cat really belonged to his daughters. Ronald Reagan (1911-1994) treasured several cats, while Bill Clinton's (1946-) black and white cat Socks became a celebrity. Socks, named after his white paws, was discovered by Chelsea Clinton as a stray kitten. He became so famous that he received large bags of fan mail and even had a diary published in 1993. According to the diary, Socks was a trifle scared by the Theodore Roosevelt lore of a Great Hunter. Even so, she broke Nancy Reagan's old china and worried the trigger-happy Secret Service men by racing up and down the hall.

Great people from other walks of life have also doted on their cats. Albert Schweitzer (1875-1965), the Nobel Prize-winning missionary, adored his pet cat Sisi, who would often perch on his shoulder while he wrote. Ernest

President Bill Clinton and First Cat of America, Socks.

Hemingway (1899-1961) lived in 907 Whitehead Street, Key West in Florida for over thirty years, during which time the house was also home to over fifty cats. Several of these had six toes, a breed of cat that was well known for hunting mice on ships during the Middle Ages. They were considered to be tokens of good fortune and for this reason had been closely associated with witchcraft. It is said that the original six-toed kitten was given to Hemingway's father by a seafaring friend of his.

T. S. Eliot (1888-1965) has been associated with cats for more than a century. Anyone who studied English literature in the 1940s and fifties will remember *Old Possum's Book of Practical Cats* (1939) that for some was a welcome contrast to his other works. It was thought to show an entirely different aspect of his character and the influence of Edward Lear. The book later became the subject of the long-running West-End musical, *Cats*.

Other writers, including Kingsley Amis (1922-1995), have enjoyed the company of their cats. Amis owned a beautiful white cat named Sarah Snow. The novellist said about cats that they 'stimulate the fancy; we weave fantasies about them'; he himself held the fantasy that Sarah Snow was learning the English language. He always maintained that people who had a cat were gentler than others. Anne Frank, (1929-1945) the diarist famously wrote of her three cats in her wartime diary, discovered and published after her death in 1946. Anne writes endearingly of the cats living in the small hideout that became home to her family during the Nazi occupation of Germany. The most extrovert of the three was Boche, who often would attack poor Tommy. However, Tommy, according to Anne, usually won in the end.

Just as in previous centuries many artists have been cat lovers. Paul Klee (1879-1940) was besotted by his cats. Henri Matisse (1869-1954) was also a great cat lover and owned a black cat. Pablo Picasso (1881-1973) had two cats and is thought to have said 'I want to make a cat like those true cats that I see crossing the road. They don't have anything in common with house pets; they have bristling fur and run like demons. If they look at you, you would say that they want to jump on your face and scratch your eyes out.' His view of the cat as wild and predatory, rather than gentle and home-loving, was clearly illustrated in his painting *Cat Chasing Bird*, painted in 1939. However outrageous the lifestyle of Andy Warhol (1928-1987), he harboured a great love of his cats, Hester and Sam. This was not known widely until after he died, when two cat books were published posthumously by his estate. Previously

Cats were popular pets with the Kennedy family, and Tom Kitten was a particular favourite.

they had printed only in small numbers.

It was an artist, who began the first national cat shows in the latter half of the nineteenth century as a way of improving the status of the cat, then definitely much lower than that of the dog. Harrison Weir is quoted as saying 'I conceived the idea that it would be well to hold 'Cat Shows', so that the different breeds, colours, markings, etc., might be more carefully attended to, and the domestic cat, sitting in front of the fire, would then possess a beauty and an attractiveness to its owner'. Weir persuaded the manager of the Crystal Palace to put one on and entered his own cat, a blue tabby called 'The Old Lady', then about fourteen years old. Weir, his brother and a clergy man, the Rev. J. Macdona, were judges at the 1871 show. Perhaps unsurprisingly, The Old Lady was judged the best in show of that colour. Cat shows took

Webster was a charmingly distinguished, large, black aristocratic feline in *The Story of Webster* by P.G. Wodehouse. So refined and poised was Webster's attitude that he made all humans feel clumsy and inept.

off. Weir wrote: 'It is to be hoped that by these shows the too often despised cat will meet with the attention and kind treatment that every dumb animal should have and ought to receive at the hands of humanity.'

Perhaps the most famous of modern cat artists is Louis Wain (1860-1939). Wain is now regarded as the most prolific as well as the most celebrated of British cat artists. Wain led a difficult and tragic life but was always comforted by his love of feline companions. After a strict upbringing, his marriage was fraught with problems. Wain's family disapproved of his wife and when she became bedridden his only joy was a black and white kitten named Peter. It was Peter that Wain began to sketch and formed the beginning of four decades of sketching and painting thousands of cats. H.G. Wells famously said of Wain that 'He made the cat his own. He invented a cat style, a cat society, a whole cat world.' Sadly, Wain spent the last fourteen years of his life in various asylums, suffering from schizophrenia. Nevertheless he did not cease his drawings and his final sketches reveal extraordinary figurative representations of cats.

Wain's devotion to his cats, which he retained even while incarcerated in a mental hospital when his mind was losing contact with reality, typifies the place cats can now hold in people's affection. In many cases they are a lifebelt in the turbulancies of the world.

The journey of the cat through history has perhaps been as curious, unpredictable and unfathomable as its nature is perceived. Few other animals have had such a diverse and complex relationship with humans. The animal that came in from the jungle to be worshipped at the altar of the ancients then suffered a reversal of fortune. From being a servant of mankind as a valued hunter of vermin, it was cruelly vilified and persecuted as Satan's agent on earth. For centuries the familiar of

Illustration of long-haired cat, from Harrison Weir's *Our Cats and All About Them*, 1889.

witches, the cat signified all that was occult and evil. And from being chivvied and tortured, it has travelled an extraordinary path to become an object of love rather than hate, acceptance rather than rejection, a pet rather than a pest. It has been a roller-coaster ride.

This traditional Louis Wain postcard bears
a curiously pertinent caption

GREAT CAT LOVERS & HATERS

CAT LOVERS

Writers and Poets

Brian Aldiss (1925-)
Cats: *Macrame, Yum-Yum, Nickie, Jackson, Foxie*

Kingsley Amis (1922-1995)
Cat: *Sarah Snow*

Matthew Arnold (1822-1888)
Cats: *Atossa, Blacky*

Honoré de Balzac (1799-1850)

Charles Baudelaire (1821-1867)

Jorge Luis Borges (1899-1986)
Cat: *Beppo*

Charlotte Brontë (1816-1855)
Cat: *Tiger*

Samuel Butler (1835-1848)

Karel Capek (1890-1938)
Cats: *Pudlenka I, II and III*

Thomas Carlyle (1795-1881)
Cat: *Columbine*

Raymond Chandler (1888-1959)
Cat: *Taki*

Jean Cocteau (1889-1963)

Colette (1893-1854)
Cats: *Ba-tou, Franchette, Kiki-la-Doucette,*
Saha, Kro, One and Only, Kapok, Muscat,
Minionne, La Chatte, La Chatte derniere, La
Touteu, Petiteu, Pinichette, Saha, Toune,
Zwerg

William Cowper (1731-1800)

Cecil Day-Lewis (1904-1972)
Cat: *Simpkin*

Charles Dickens (1812-1870)
Cats: *William/Williamina; the Master's Cat*

Alexandre Dumas (1824-1895)
Cats: *Mysouff I and II, le Docteur*

T. S. Eliot (1888-1965)
Cats: *Noilly Prat, Pattipaws, Pushdragon, Tantomile, Wiscus*

Anatole France (1844-1924)
Cats: *Hamilcar, Pascal*

Anne Frank (1929-1945)
Cats: *Boche, Mouschi, Tommy*

Théophile Gautier (1811-1872)
Cats: *Childebrand, Cléopâtre, Eponine, Zizi, Enjolras, Madame Théophile, Don Perrot de Navarre, Gavroche, Seraphita*

Thomas Hardy (1840-1928)
Cat: *Cobby*

Ernest Hemmingway (1899-1961)
Owned many cats including *Crazy Christian, Dillinger, Ecstasy, Fats, Furhouse, Friendless Brother, Thruster*

Victor Hugo (1802-1885)
Cats: *Gavroche, Mouche*

Leigh Hunt (1784-1859)

Aldous Huxley (1894-1963)

Henry James (1843-1916)

Jerome K Jerome (1859-1927)

Samuel Johnson (1709-1784)
Cats: *Hodge, Lilly*

Michael Joseph (1897-1958)
Cats: *Charles, Minna Minna Mobray*

John Keats (1795-1821)

Rudyard Kipling (1865-1936)

Doris Lessing (1919-)

Bernard Levin (1928-)

Compton Mackenzie (1883-1972)
Cats: *Sylvia, Pippo, Tootloose*

Don Marquis (1878-1937)

Guy de Maupassant (1850-1893)

Michel de Montaigne (1533-1592)
Cat: *Madame Vanity*

Iris Murdoch (1919-1999)
Cat: *General Butchkin*

Petrarch (1304-1374)

Edgar Allen Poe (1811-1849)
Cat: *Catarina*

Gabriel Rossetti (1783-1954)
Cat: *Zoe*

Georges Sand (1804-1876)

Cat: *Minou*

Dorothy L. Sayers (1893-1958)
Cat: *Timothy*

Sir Walter Scott (1771-1832)
Cat: *Hinse*

Percy Bysshe Shelley (1792-1822)

Edith Sitwell (1887-1964)

Christopher Smart (1722-1771)

Robert Southey (1774-1843)
Cats: *Bona Marietta, Pulcheria, Sir
Thomas Dido, The Zombi*

Sir Roy Strong (1935-)
Cat: *The Reverend Wenceslas Muff*

William Makepeace Thackeray
(1811-1863)
Cat: *Louisa*

Mark Twain (1835-1910)
Cats: *Apollinaris, Blatherskite, Sour Mash,
Zoroaster*

Paul Verlaine (1844-1896)

Horace Walpole (1717-1797)
Cats: *Fatima, Harold, Selima, Patapan,
Zara*

H.G. Wells (1866-1946)
Cat: *Mr Peter Wells*

William Wordsworth (1770-1850)

William Butler Yeats (1865-1939)

Emile Zola (1840-1902)

Artists

Jean Auguste Dominique Ingres (1780-1867)
Cats: *Patrocle, Procope*

Paul Klee (1879-1940)
Cats: *Bimbo, Fritzi, Myz, Nuggi*

Edward Lear (1812-1888)
Cat: *Foss*

Leonardo da Vinci (1452-1519)

Edward Manet (1832-1883)

Henri Matisse (1869-1954)

Pablo Picasso (1881-1973)
Siamese

Stanley Spencer (1891-1959)

Louis Wain (1860-1939)

Andy Warhol (1928-1987)
Cats: *Hester and Sam*

James McNeill Whistler (1834-1903)

Composers

Alexander Borodin (1833-1887)
Cats: *Fisherman, Longy, Tommy*

Frederic Chopin (1810-1849)

Jean Michel Jarre (1948-)

Domenico Scarlatti (1685-1757)
Cat: *Pulcinella*

Sir Andrew Lloyd Webber (1948-)

Actors and Actresses

Ann-Margaret (1941-)
Cats: *Big Red, Tuffy*

Fred Astaire (1899-1987)
One black cat

Tallulah Bankhead (1903-1968)
Lion cub

Brigitte Bardot (1934-)
Sixty cats

Kim Basinger (1953-)

Warren Beatty (1937-)

Doris Day (1924-)
Ten cats, including *Punky*

Melanie Griffith (1957-)

Charles Laughton (1889-1962)

Janet Leigh (1927-)
Cat: *Turkey*

Vivien Leigh (1913-1967)
Cats: *Boy, New*

James Mason (1909-1984)

Robert de Niro (1943-)
Seven cats

Beryl Reid (1920-1996)
Cat: *Cleopatra, Dimly, Lulu*

Elizabeth Taylor (1932-)
Three cats

Franco Zeffirelli (1923-)
One Persian

Scientists and Philosophers

Jeremy Bentham (1748-1832)
Cat: *The Reverend Sir John Langbourne DD*

Erasmus Darwin (1731-1802)
Cat: *Persian Snow*

Albert Einstein (1879-1955)

Thomas Huxley (1825-1895)

Isaac Newton (1642-1727)

Albert Schweitzer (1875-1965)
Cat: *Sizi*

Leaders and Heads of State

Jimmy Carter (1924-)
Cats: *Misty Malarky Ying Yang*

King Charles I (1600-1649)
One black cat

Emperor Chu Hou-Tsung of China (1507-1566)
Cat: *Frost Eyebrows*

Sir Winston Churchill (1874-1965)
Cats: *Jock, Margate, Nelson, Tango (aka Mr Cat)*

Bill Clinton (1946-)
Cat: *Socks*

Calvin Coolidge (1872-1933)
Cats: *Blackie, Smokey, Tiger and Timmy*

King Edward VII (1841-1910)
Manx cats

Gerald Ford (1913-)
Cat: *Shan*

Pope Gregory I (540-604)

Rutherford B. Hayes (1822-1873)
Cat: *Siam*

Paul von Hindenberg (1847-1934)

Emperor Ichijo of Japan (986-1011)
Cat: *Myobu No Omoto*

John F. Kennedy (1917-1963)
Cat: *Tom Kitten*

Pope Leo XII (1760-1829)
Cat: *Micetto*

Abraham Lincoln (1809-1865)
Cat: *Tabby*

Louis XIII of France (1601-1643)

Louise XV of France (1710-1774)

Mohammad (570-632)
Cat: *Muezza*

Pope Pius IX (1792-1878)

Ronald Reagan (1911-2004)
Cats: *Cleo and Sara*

Cardinal Richelieu (1585-1642)
Cats: *Soumise, Sepolet, Mimie Paillon, Felimare, Lucifer, Lodoviska, Rubis sur l'Ongle, Pyrame, Thisbe, Racan, Perruque*

Theodore Roosevelt (1859-1919)
Cats: *Slippers, Tom Quartz*

Queen Victoria (1819-1901)
Cat: *White Heather*

Harold Wilson (1916-1995)
Cat: *Memo*

Cardinal Thomas Wolsey (1471-1530)

GREAT CAT HATERS

Alexander the Great (356-323)
Alexander is said to have hated cats
so much that he swooned at the
sight of one.

Hilaire Belloc (1870-1953)
'So utterly lacking are They in
simplicity and humility, and so
abominably well filled with cunning
by whatever demon first brought
Their race into existence. All
that They do is venomous, and
all that They think is evil.'

Johannes Brahms (1833-1897)
Brahms would shoot them from his
window with a sparrow-slaying bow,
given to him as a gift by Dvořák.

Julius Caesar (100-44 BC)
Julius Caesar loathed cats and
would order their immediate death
if he set eyes on one.

Isadora Duncan (1878-1927)
Isadora Duncan, the American
dancer, lived next door to a
countess who ran a cat sanctuary at
Neuilly, France. Detesting cats
Duncan ordered her staff to 'Hunt
them down and drown them all'.

Dwight Eisenhower (1890-1969)
Eisenhower hated cats and banished
them from the White House,
instructing his staff, 'Make sure you
shoot any cat on sight'.

Elizabeth I (1533-1603)
At Queen Elizabeth I's coronation,
according to the custom of the day,
a large basket filled with live cats
formed part of the procession
through the streets. The basket was
set on fire and the cats burned

to death during the proceedings.

Pope Gregory IX (1147-1241)
In the Papal Bull of 1233 Pope
Gregory decreed that the cat was
derived from the devil himself and
gave his blessing to the persecution
of cats that was to continue for five
centuries.

Abdul Hamid (1725-1789)
The great Ottoman Sultan felt a
terror of cats and could not stand
any to be within sight or sound of
his great palaces.

Henri II (1551-1589)
The French King put 30,000 cats
to death during his reign and is said
to have lost consciousness if he
caught sight of one.

King Louis XIV (1638-1715)
In 1648 the ten-year-old Louis set
alight pyres of cats to be burned
alive at the Midsummer Gala in the
Place de Grève in Paris, then danced
around them.

Napoleon Bonaparte (1769-1821)
The Emperor Napoleon was highly
allergic to cats, his eyes would well
up with tears if he happened to be
in the same room with people who
had been in contact with cats a few
hours earlier.

Wu-Chao, Empress (624-705)
Wu-Chao, the Empress of China,
hated cats after a lady-in-waiting
that she had condemned to death
issued a curse before she died. The
lady-in-waiting promised to turn
the Empress into a rat and hound
her
as a cat.

SELECT BIBLIOGRAPHY

Aberconway, Christabel, *A Dictionary of Cat Lovers: XV Century BC to XX Century AD*, Michael Joseph, 1949

Aldrovandus, *Natural History of Quadrupeds*, A. Asher, Amsterdam, 1980

Altman, Roberta, *The Quintessential Cat*, Macmillan, New York, 1994

Ash, R., *Dear Cats. The Post Office Letters*, Pavilion, London 1986

Baudelaire, Charles, *Les Fleurs du Mal*, Blackwell, Oxford, 1980

Berwick, Thomas, *A General History of Quadrupeds*, London, 1790

Boylan, Clare, *The Literary Companion to Cats*, Sinclair-Stevenson, 1995

Briggs, Katharine, *Nine Lives: Cats in Folklore*, Routledge/Kegan Paul, 1980

Burn. B, *The Morris Approach*, 1980

Carroll, Lewis, *Alice Through the Looking Glass*, and *Alice in Wonderland*, Macmillan, 1871 and 1865 respectively

Clutton-Brock, Juliet, *The British Museum Book of Cats*, British Museum Publications, London, 1988

Cole, W. and Ungerer, T. *A Cat-Hater's Handbook*, W.H. Allen, London, 1963

Cox, N. and Povey, D. *A Picasso Bestiary*, Academic Editions, London, 1995

Daniels, M., *Morris: An Intimate Biography*, William Morrow, 1974

Davies, Marion, *The Magical Lore of Cats*, Capall Bann, Berks, 1995

De Laroche, Robert and Labat, Jean-Michel, *The Secret Life of Cats*, Aurum Press, London, 1993

Fleury-Husson, Jules (pseudonym M.Champfleury), *Les Chats; Histoire, Meours, Observations, Anecdotes*, 1869

Fogle B, *The Cat's Mind: Understanding Your Pet's Behaviour*, Pelham Books, 1991

Greene, David, *Incredible Cats*, Methuen, London, 1995

Grilhe, Gillette, *The Cat and Man*, Putnam's, New York, 1974

Harris, *The Renowned History of the White Cat*, London, 1803

Hopkins, M., *Discovery of Witches*, 1647

Howey, M. Oldfield, *The Cat in the Mysteries of Religion and Magic*, Rider, 1930

Huet, J.B. *Collection des Mammifères du Muséum d'Histoire Naturelle*, Paris, 1808

Jardine, William, *The Natural History of the Felinae*, 1834

Johnstonus, Johannes, *Historaie Naturalis*, 1657

Kirk, Mildred, *The Everlasting Cat*, The Overlook Press, Woodstock, 1977

Kohen, Elli, *World History and Myths of Cats*, The Edwin Mellen Press, 2003

Lear, Edward, *The Heraldic Blazon of Foss the Cat*, 1884

Loxton, Howard, *Cats in History, Legend and Literature*, Chronicle Books, San Fransisco, 1988

Marks, Anne, *The Cat in History, Legend and Art*, Elliot Stock, London, 1909

Moncrif, Francois Augustin Paradis de, *Les Chats*, 1727

Montgomery, J., *Arthur the Television Cat*, WH Allen, London 1975
Morris, Desmond, *Catworld*, Ebury Press, London, 1996

Necker, Claire, *The Natural History of Cats*, Delta, New York, 1970

Pond, Grace, ed. *The Complete Cat Encyclopedia*, Heinemann, London, 1972

Repplier, Agnes, *The Fireside Sphinx*, Gay and Bird, London, 1901
Ross, Charles H, *The Book of Cats*, 1868

Simpson, Frances, *The Book of the Cat*, Cassell, 1903

Steinlen, T., *Des Chats - Images sans Paroles*, 1890

Suares, J.C. *The Indispensable Cat*, Webb & Bower, Exeter, 1984

Tabor, Roger, *Cats: The Rise of the Cat*, BBC Books, London, 1991

Topsell, Edward, *History of Four-footed Beasts and Serpents*, 1658

Van Vechten, Carl, *The Tiger in the House*, Knopf, New York, 1920

Weir, Harrison, *Our Cats and All About Them*, 1889

Wheen, Francis, *The Chatto Book of Cats*, Chatto & Windus Ltd, London, 1993